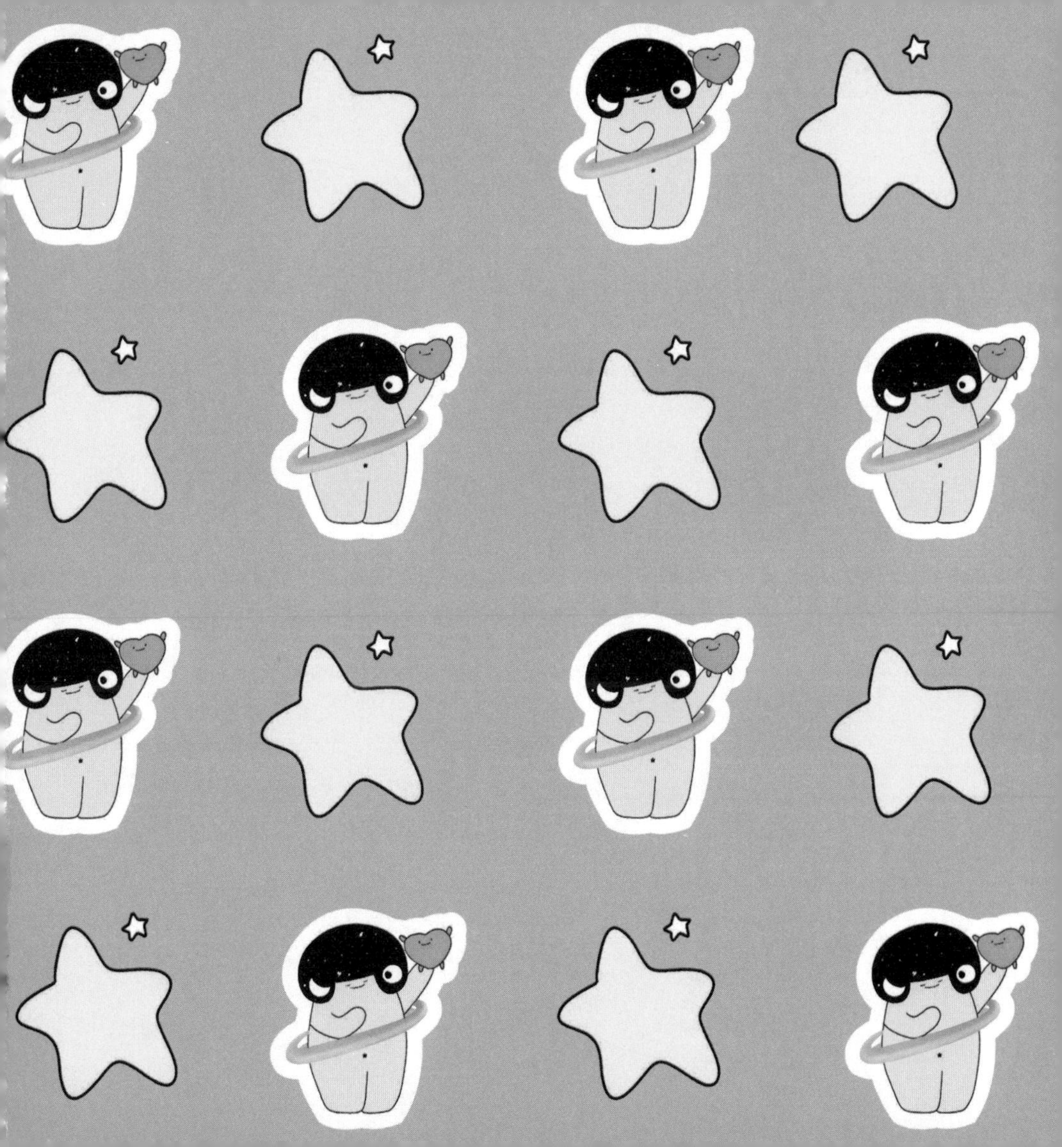

I BELIEVE IN ME

I BELIEVE IN ME

Finding Joy with Heartwarming Affirmations

Cheng Chi Sing, also known as Soolooka

mango
PUBLISHING GROUP

CORAL GABLES

Published by Mango Publishing Group, a division of Mango Media Inc.

Cover Design: Elina Diaz
Cover illustration: Cheng Chi Sing
Layout & Design: Elina Diaz

For permission requests, please contact the publisher at:
Mango Publishing Group
2850 S Douglas Road, 2nd Floor
Coral Gables, FL 33134 USA
info@mango.bz

For special orders, quantity sales, course adoptions and corporate sales, please email the publisher at sales@mango.bz. For trade and wholesale sales, please contact Ingram Publisher Services at customer.service@ingramcontent.com or +1.800.509.4887.

I Believe in Me: Finding Joy with Heartwarming Affirmations

Library of Congress Cataloging-in-Publication number: 2020939619
ISBN: (print) 978-1-64250-309-8, (ebook) 978-1-64250-310-4
BISAC category code: SEL021000—SELF-HELP / Motivational & Inspirational

Printed in the United States of America

To you, beautiful souls

Table of Contents

Foreword   **11**

Introduction   **13**

Chapter 1: **I Will Make It Through the Bad Times Stronger Than Before**   **20**

Chapter 2: **There Is Always a Way Out**   **47**

Chapter 3: **I Am Worthy—I Was Born Worthy**   **82**

Chapter 4: **Good Days Are on Their Way**   **113**

Chapter 5: **I Can Do It**   **144**

Chapter 6: **I Promise Myself...**   **175**

Chapter 7: **Affirmations**   **205**

Conclusion   **241**

Acknowledgments   **243**

About the Author   **244**

Foreword

When life gets tough, it's hard to know what steps you can take to improve your mental health and well-being. So often, common advice is invalidating and less-than-helpful; "Just smile and things feel better." "You sound ungrateful, be grateful for what you have." "Stop thinking about the bad things, be positive!" These platitudes, at best, cause a feeling of annoyance, and at worst, feelings of shame and alienation.

Unfortunately, a lot of the advice that people give and receive regarding mental health struggles are these kinds of dismissive hand-waves. While well-meaning, they offer little practical use and can often lead to further frustration or isolation, as they treat very real problems as inconveniences to be ignored or disregarded rather than what they are: obstacles to be overcome.

Soolooka's work offers a wonderful solution to this problem. Instead of dismissing mental health struggles, Soolooka faces them head-on. She does this by distilling tried-and-true mental health rituals and coping mechanisms into welcoming cartoons that kindly encourage you to become the healthiest version of you. And where mental health "homework" you might receive from a therapist can feel dry or overwhelming, Soolooka's clever work helps to make these exercises feel both doable and approachable. With each and every cartoon, she offers actual, concrete solutions to various challenges.

You never have to feel alone in your struggles to become mentally resilient. With kindness and compassion, *I Believe in Me* will always be here for you.

Kate Allan
Author of *You Can Do All Things*, *Thera-Pets*, and
It's Your Weirdness That Makes You Wonderful

Introduction

You may not be able to tell from my drawings, but I wasn't always a happy person. I used to overthink so much that I annoyed even myself. "What will they think of me?" "Am I doing this well enough to make everyone happy?" "Why did I say that, she seems upset now?" I felt I was neither perfect enough to be liked by everybody, nor broken enough to have the people in my life concerned about me. In other words, I was just normal, ordinary, mediocre, boring—any average term, you name it. Still, I wanted to show the best part of me to the world, the part that I thought others would love to see. So I tried very hard to be accepted by others, constantly seeking approval. I was always busy being the *best* me—even when I was alone, because I needed to practice. It was tiring, but I guessed life was just like that; everyone had their own problems.

That was the old, sad me. Do you feel the same way I did?

Now I draw every weekday and share my work on Instagram—healing my heart with art, sharing my insights about life, and expressing my sincere feelings with the world, in the hopes people are inspired by my illustrations and words. I am grateful to be able to help. Every day, my platform,

Soolooka, reaches more and more people. This is magical, too magical, considering that this wasn't my plan at all—going on a self-love journey, being a self-love illustrator, making friends with beautiful souls around the world.

"You don't have any talent in art, unlike your sister, she draws great." This is what my mother has always told me, even now.

While many people comment positively about my drawing style, saying it is cute and that I am talented, I often feel embarrassed (but thankful, too) because of the conflict between their praise and my old belief. Before I started to share my work online, I didn't really draw, and I didn't have any formal training in art or design. Because I was regarded as an untalented child in art at home, I wouldn't draw unless it was related to a class or homework. Being an author has always been my dream, but an illustrator? "Hmmm, maybe it's not my thing," I would say to myself.

In the last few years, I had been interested in learning more about myself and the root of all my anxieties. I read books and joined workshops. I knew I needed a change, but change isn't fun at all. The "knowing myself" journey was very intense and painful. Sometimes I wished I never knew the truth, and went back to the old, sad me. Other times, I strived for transformation.

After I decided to quit my job and take a break, I started to think about what to do next that I would love or that would contribute to the world, or at least a small group of people. "Learn illustration and share what you've learned from the past and in everyday life!" said a loud voice inside of me—it's funny that the voice didn't come from my head, but my heart. "Oh wow, but that sounds scary," another voice inside my brain replied. The thought of showing others the thoughts of a nobody and drawings from an "untalented" person froze me. My face turned red and I began to sweat as if I was running under the big, hot sun.

I had always been a loyal fan of my brain, following the SHOULDs that it instructed me, instead of what my heart asked for tenderly. "I should study in university, it doesn't matter what major I choose, people say having a degree is important." "I should get a job right after I graduate from university, because I should bring home the bacon, though a grad trip with friends would be super nice." "I should not quit my job because my parents don't think I should quit." "I should continue to work in a stable environment, and get promoted, just like most people do. But...what about my purpose in life?" "I should get married and have kids so that my parents don't need to worry about me." "I should go to my friend's party, though I want to stay home."

For the very first time, I heard my "heart voice" so loudly that I couldn't ignore it anymore. At the same time, I was super fearful of what would happen next if I followed my heart. What if people hated what I shared? What if my friends teased me about it?

"Just do it anyway!" my heart said firmly. "Well, okay, whatever happens won't kill me," I guessed, so I decided to take the leap. And here I am today. I now know I don't need to be perfect to be amazing, I don't need to outsource validation, I don't need to pretend to be someone to be loved. I also know that I can be the biggest supporter of myself. And you can, too.

That's why I wrote this little book. With hope that the messages from my heart can support you through the difficult seasons in your life, to help you to learn to see your worthiness, and help you turn self-love and self-care into habits.

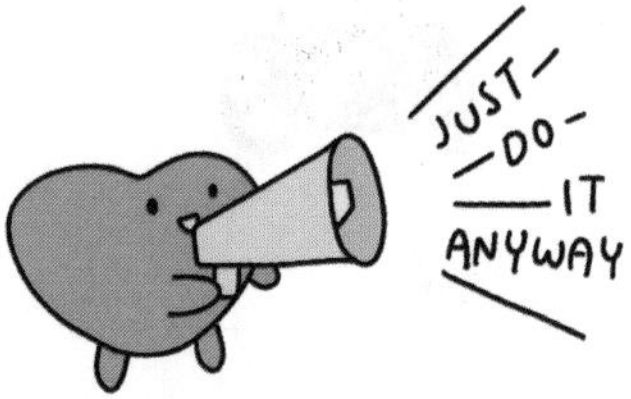
JUST
DO
IT
ANYWAY

How many times have we listened and believed what others said, without trying to experience our own life first?

How many times have we forced ourselves to do something we thought we *should* do, and let down our heart?

How many times have we regretted not taking the opportunities that came our way and missed out some important things in life?

And how many times more do we want these things to happen again and again?

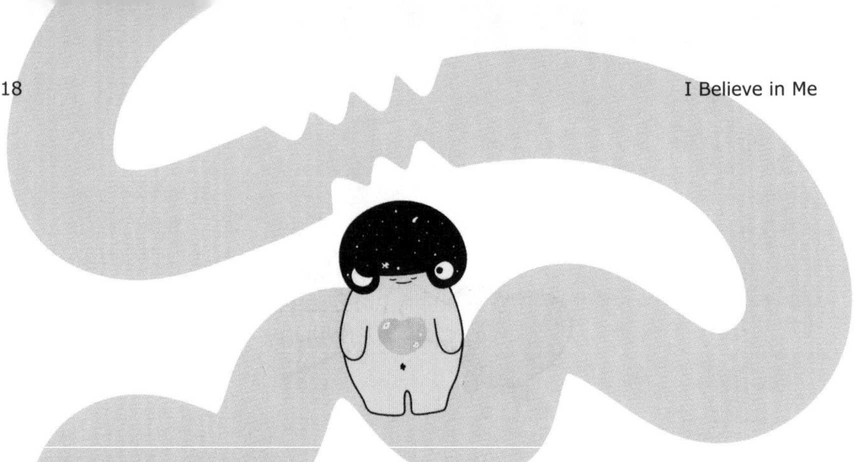

There is power and magic inside every one of us (you may not notice it yet, but trust me, you will find it as you read through this book). You can transform your life into a more shiny and joyful one whenever you are ready. Life may not be as easy a journey as we wish it to be, but it is definitely a beautiful one our soul is longing for. Challenges will be there for us, pain is inevitable in growth, but sweet fruit is promised at the end.

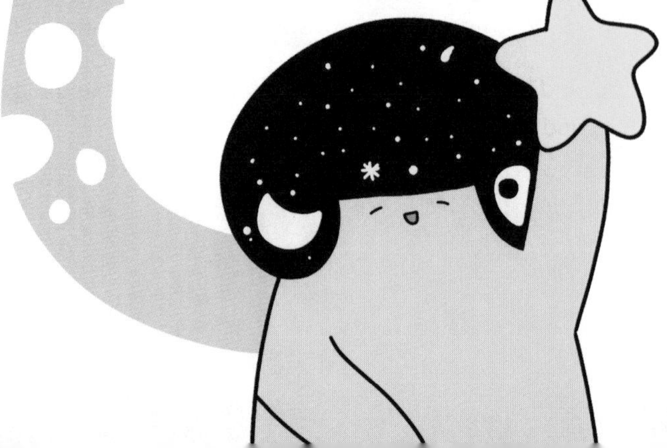

This book cannot teach you how to solve every problem in your life, but it includes the messages my own heart tells me when I am experiencing dark times. You are not alone, because I am with you. I am sending you lots of love and good vibes through my drawings and words. I hope the illustrations and exercises in this book can give you a boost when you feel sad, stressed, or anxious.

May we now start our self-love journey together, brave souls!

CHAPTER ONE

I WILL MAKE IT THROUGH THE BAD TIMES STRONGER THAN BEFORE

-when you are in those bad days-

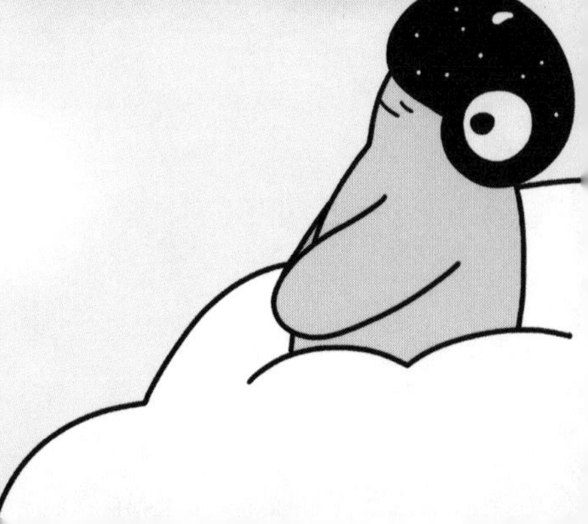

When You Are in Those Bad Days

We all love good days, when everything is going well, the air we breathe is sweet, people talk like music, we can feel the sun floating among the clouds, and even a dog's bark can make our day. Just like anything, however, good days come and go. Sometimes we have bad days, when the heaviness of our heart makes it difficult to breathe, our mood becomes a shadow hanging over us, and we don't know how to shut up the everlasting negative self-talk in our head.

People love to talk about positivity these days, but sometimes this can make us feel like it's *wrong* to feel bad. We want to maintain our professional appearance at work, we don't want our family to worry about us, maybe we just don't want anyone to know that we are not okay—including ourselves. No one wants to be a negative person, we don't *want* bad days, but what can we do?

Life is a cycle, and everything in it too. Bad days come, and will eventually go. Remember that after winter, there comes spring. First, however, we have to survive winter—even though it's rough and we are not having fun at all. If you are wondering whether or not you are tough enough to survive it, the answer is YES. Life never gives us challenges that we can't handle.

Being strong is not the only way to ease our days—accepting our own vulnerability can lead us to the door of happiness, too.

We have to recognize how we feel before we can be healed, however. People ask me why this step is important, why they can't just ignore the negative emotions and move on. As much as we might want to rid ourselves of the bad feelings, however, it won't work this way.

All of us know how destructive dark thoughts can be; they may hurt our relationships with others, or make us do things that we later regret. The more energy we give them, the more powerful the negative emotions will be. Many of us then choose to suppress them—because of social norms, our experience, our beliefs, or the behavior we model from our parents— thinking that if we do this, they will go away. What we don't know is that burying the negative emotions is like turning the destructive weapon from pointing outward to inward. This will drain and eventually consume us.

The thing is, emotions are here to tell us something, whether we want to hear it or not. Acknowledging and facing them is the best way to resolve them. To listen to them without judgment, and to accept that the emotions are valid, without clinging to them so that they can control us. We are not our emotions, but we *can* accept that we all have them. It's okay to have bad days, and it's okay to feel bad. Just have faith that all is well, and everything will be okay.

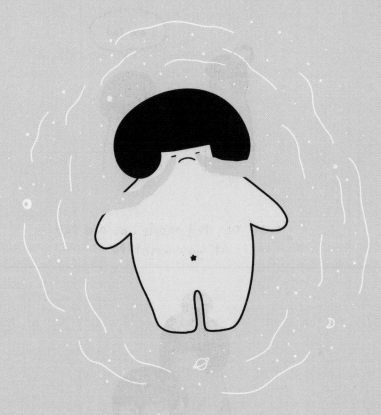

it's okay to cry......
in shower, in bed, in public, in front of your loved ones
it's okay to cry

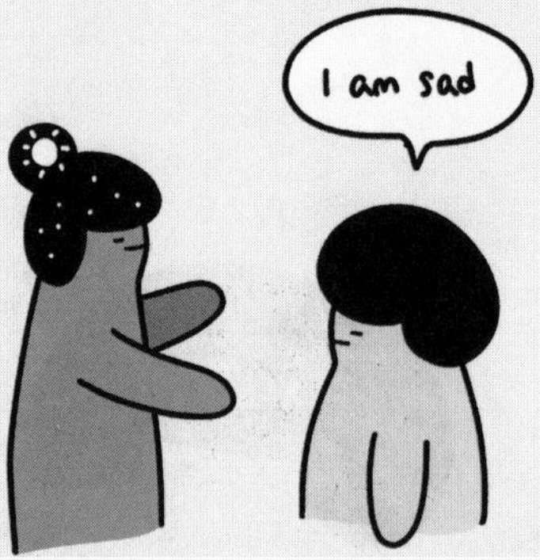
I am sad

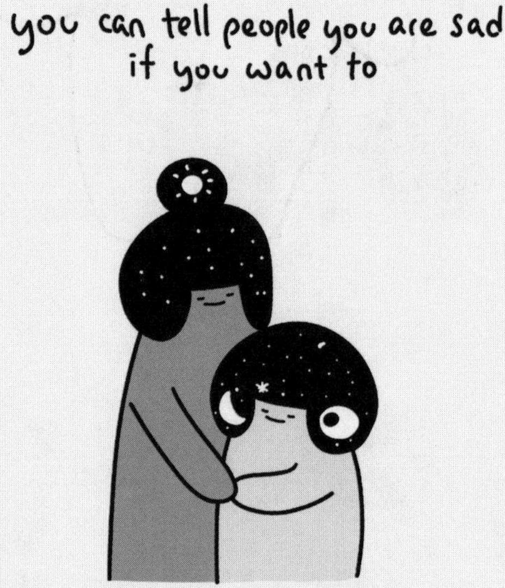
you can tell people you are sad
if you want to

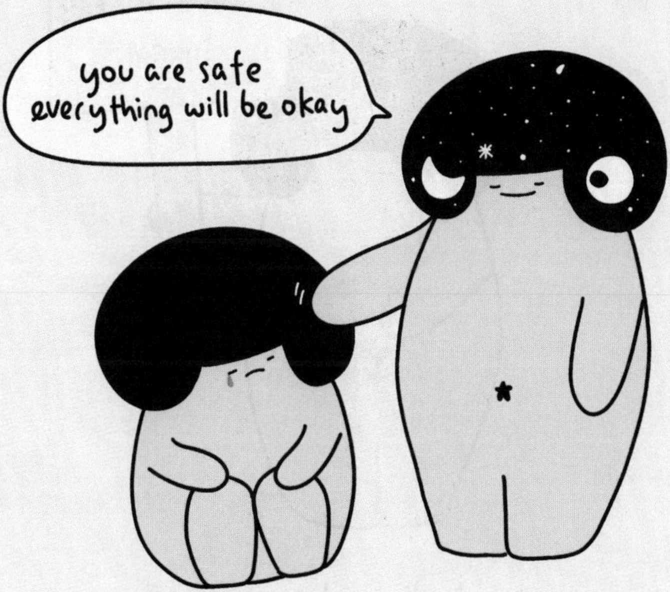
you are safe
everything will be okay

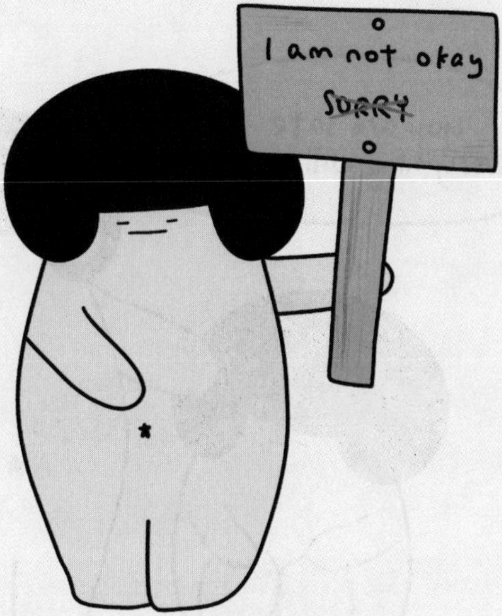
I am not okay
SORRY

you don't need to apologise
for feeling not okay
to others and yourself too

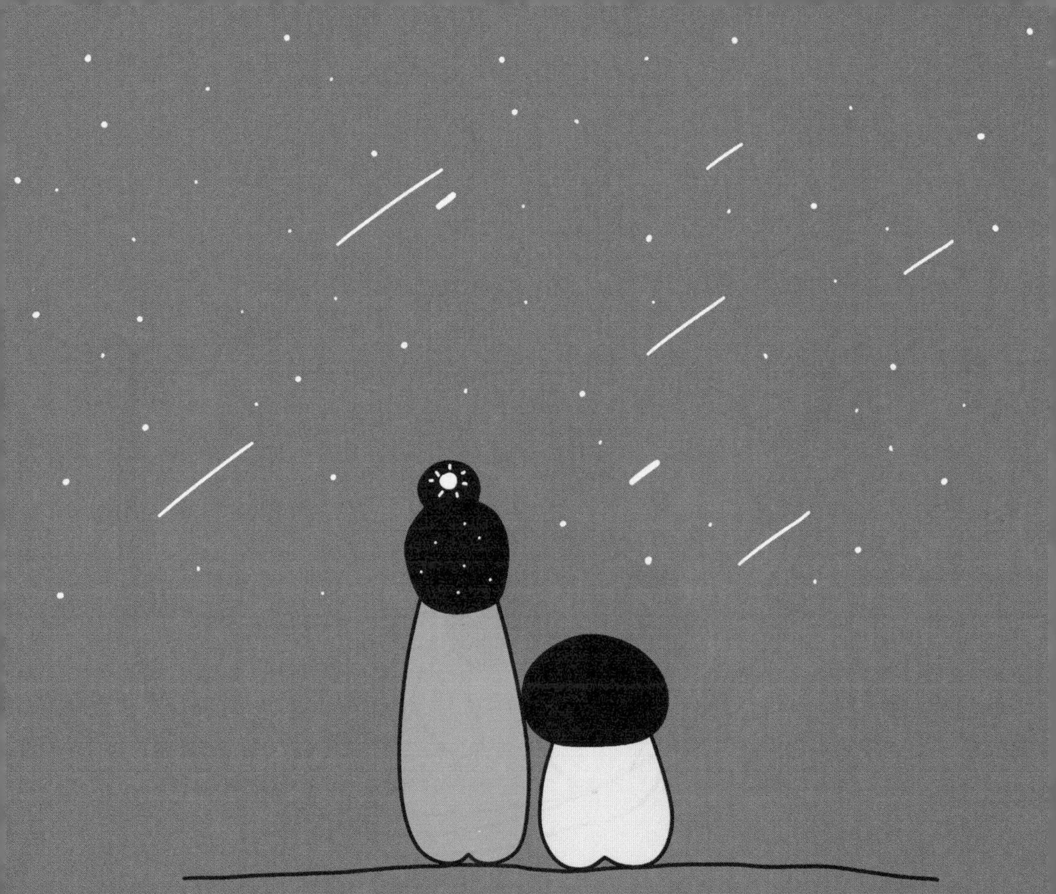

It's okay to talk to a friend, or not,
just have a friend accompany you

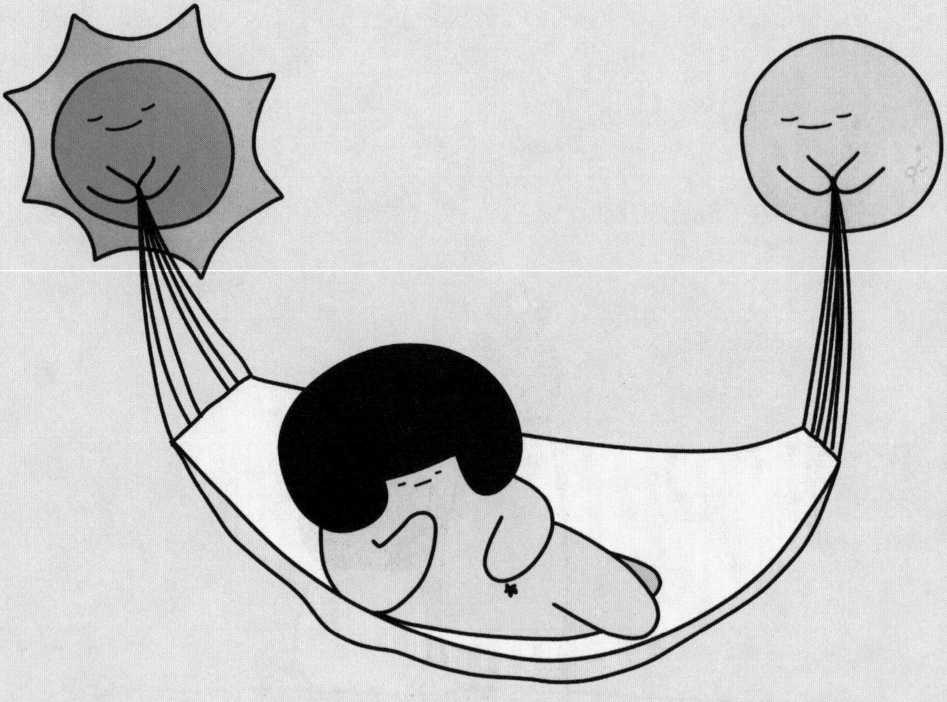

If you need time to be alone
take your time

you can drop the things that
make you feel bad

Be happy!!
I am not going to force happiness, I'll create it in my own way

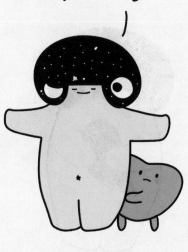

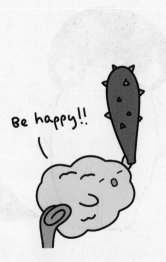

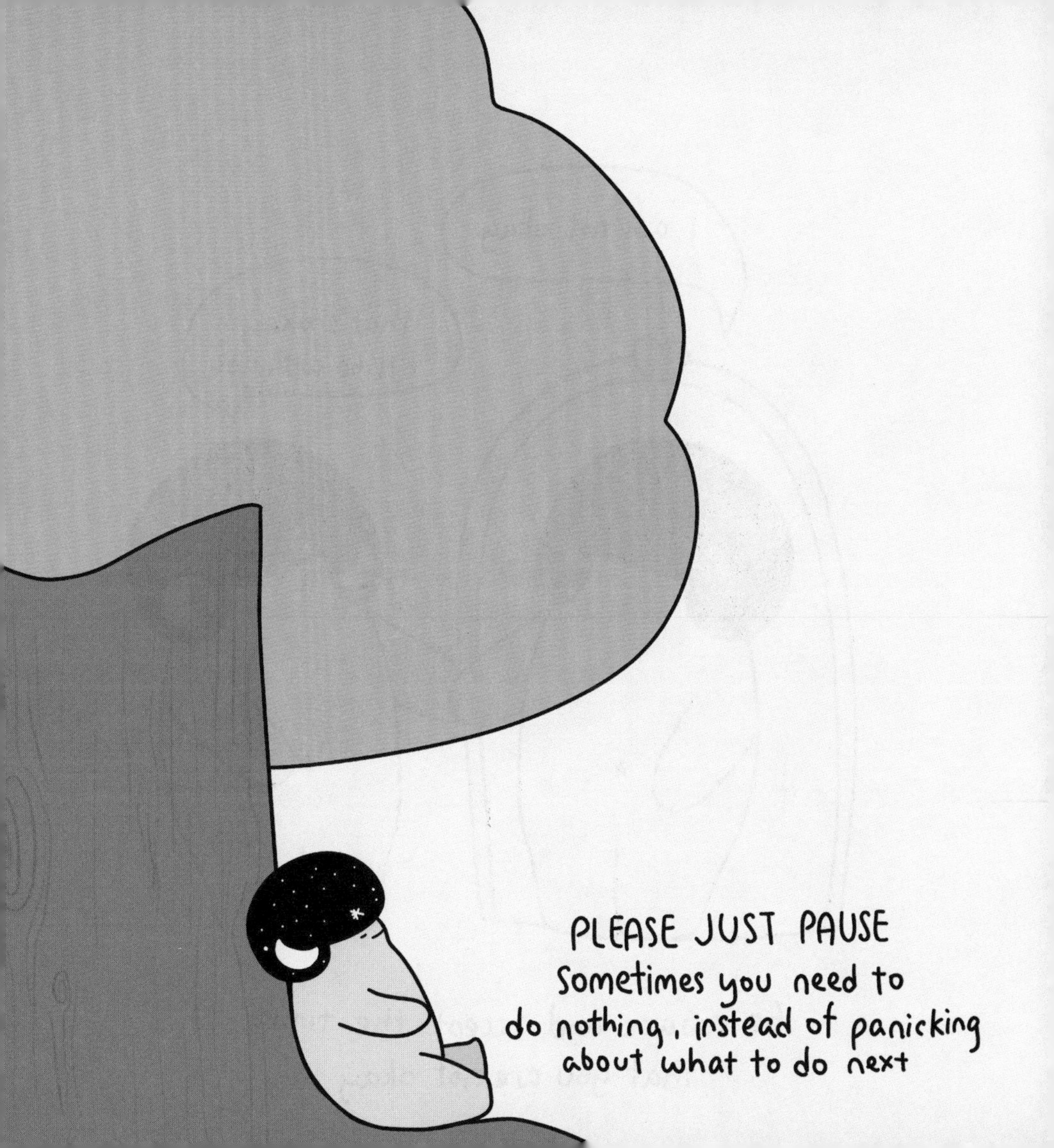
PLEASE JUST PAUSE
Sometimes you need to
do nothing, instead of panicking
about what to do next

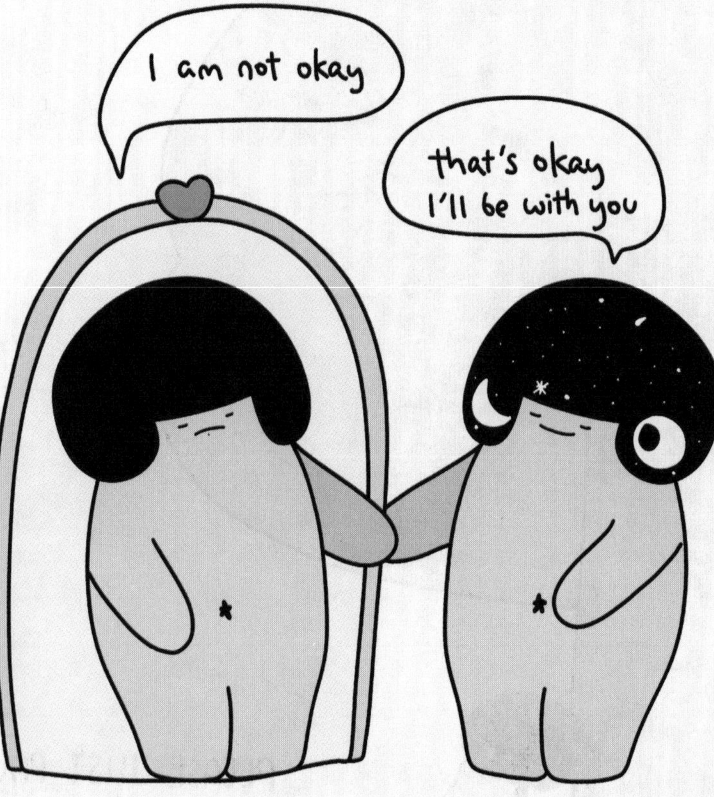
I am not okay
that's okay
I'll be with you

be aware and accept the times
that you are not okay

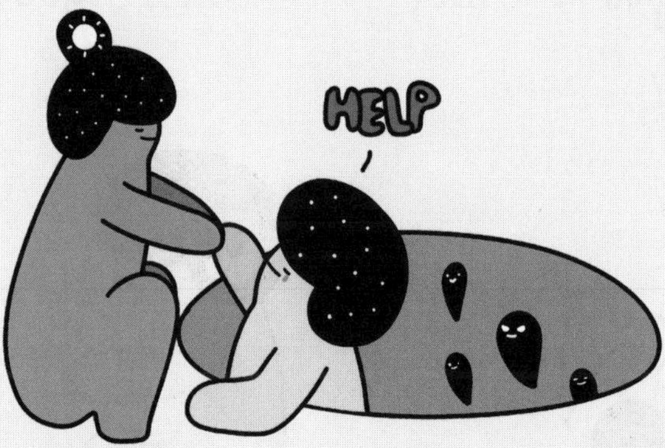
HELP

reach out

there's always someone willing to help

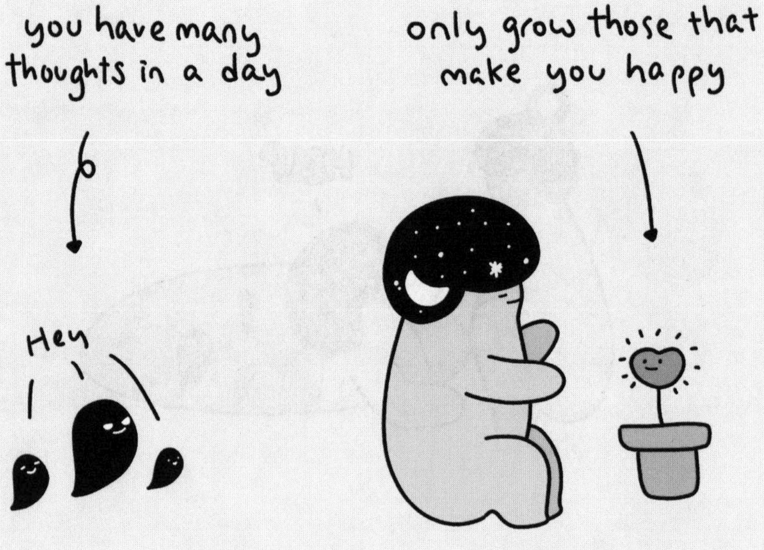
you have many thoughts in a day
Hey
only grow those that make you happy

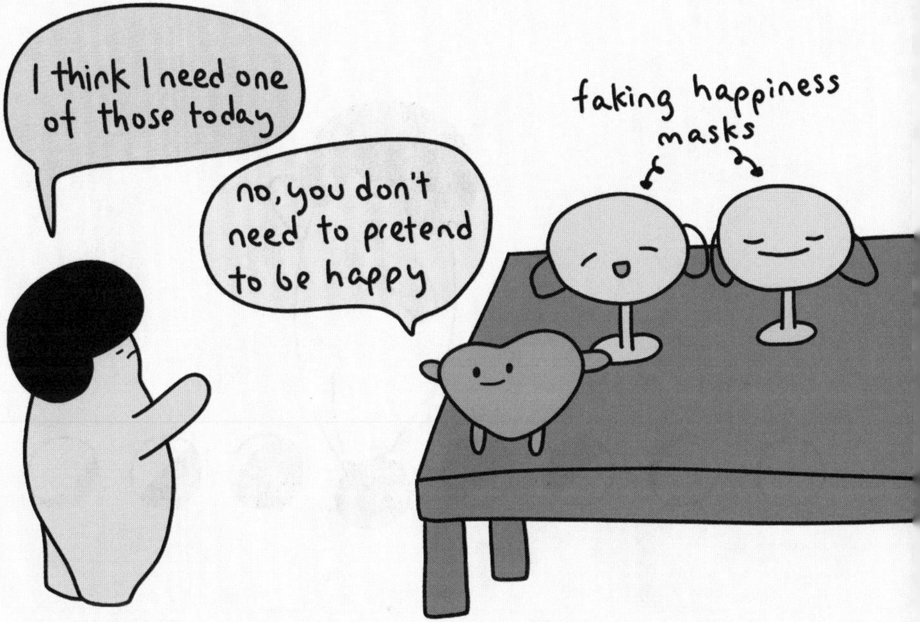
I think I need one of those today
no, you don't need to pretend to be happy
faking happiness masks

tough times are temporary
remember, one step at a time

It's okay to have good time
in bad days
You are allowed to be happy

you survived bad days in the past

you'll survive the bad days now and in the future

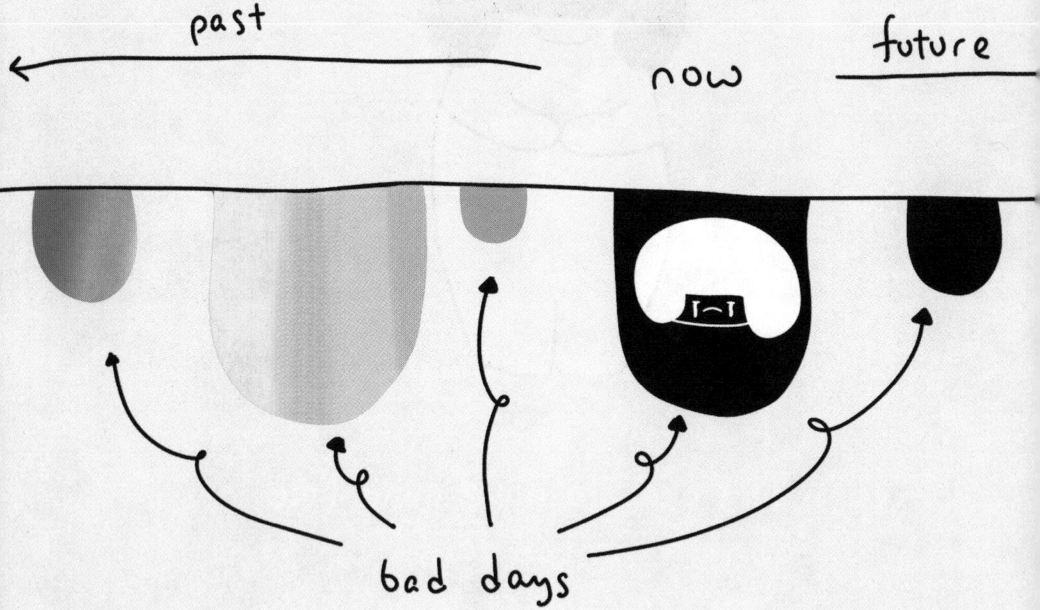
past
now
future
bad days

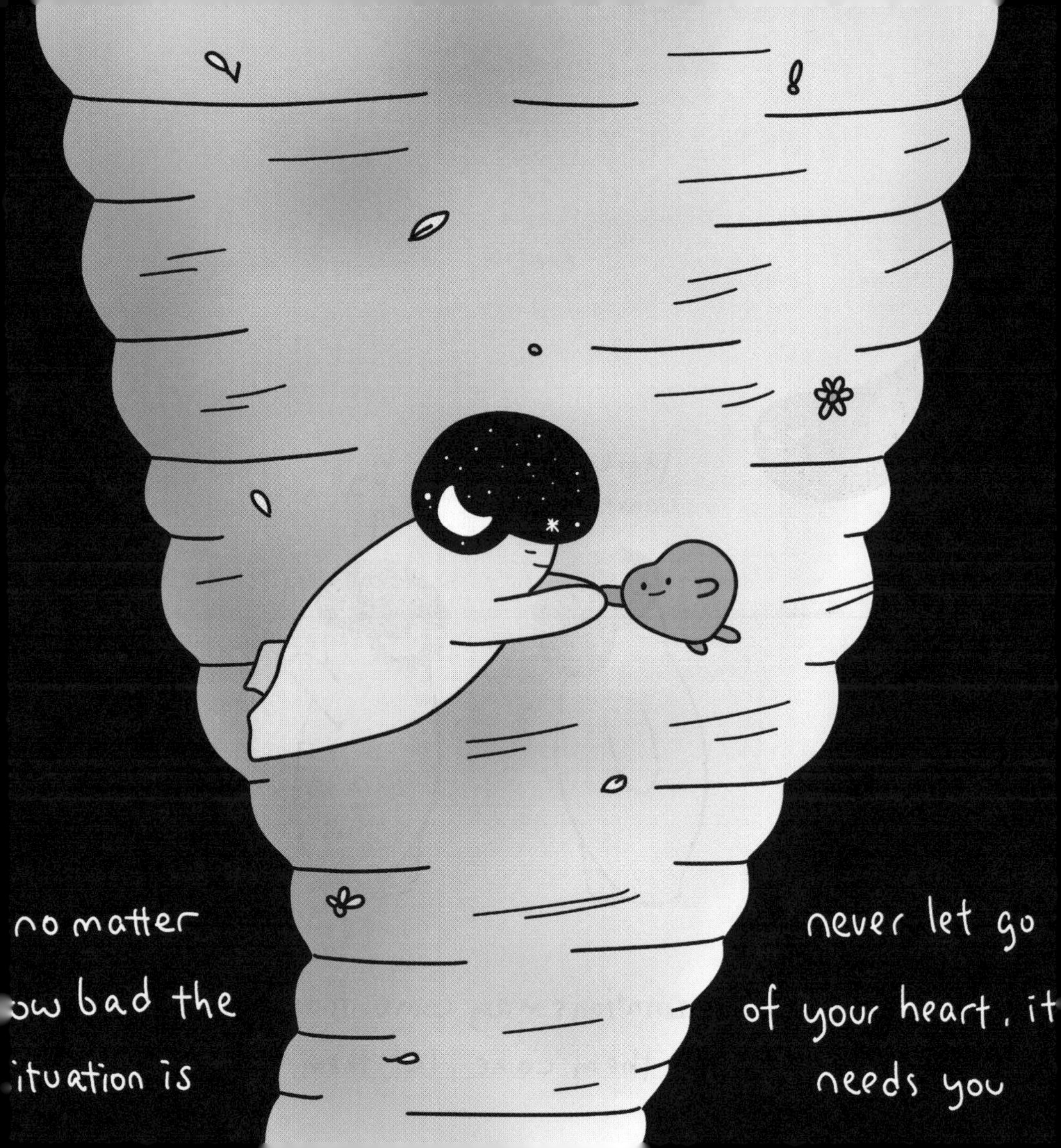
no matter
ow bad the
ituation is
never let go
of your heart, it
needs you

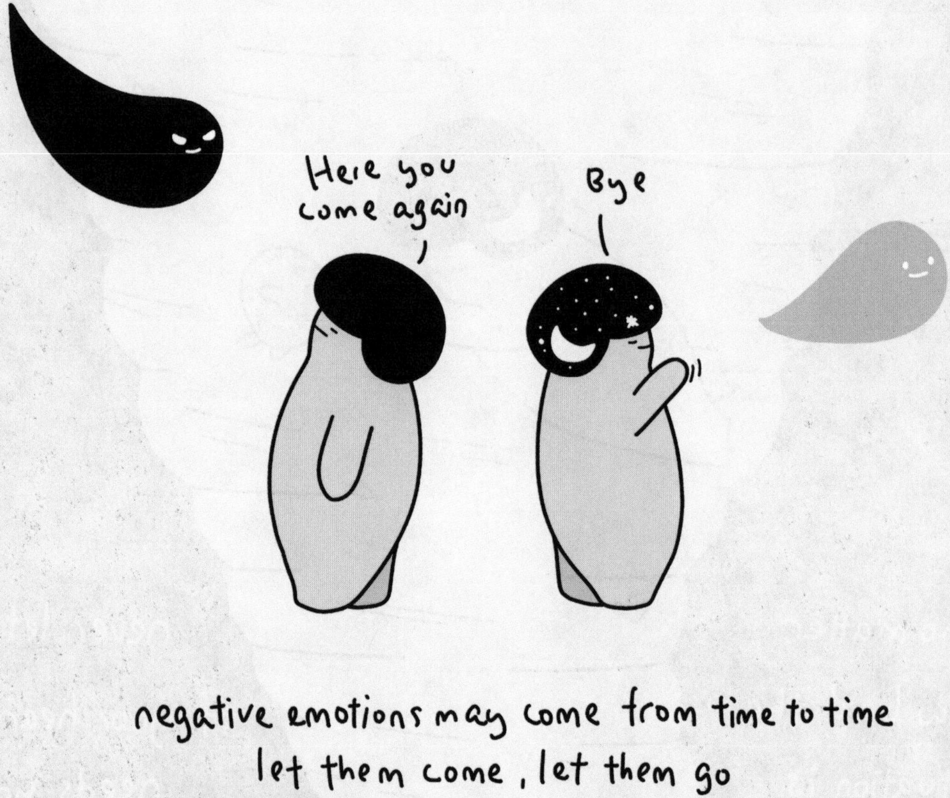
Here you come again
Bye
negative emotions may come from time to time
let them come, let them go

While being positive can be really difficult on a bad day, choosing positivity is possible. Find the light in the dark days, no matter how small it is—it will warm your heart. It may not be easy at first, especially when you are sad and tired. But I encourage you to make yourself *want* to do so, simply because of the fact that you deserve love and joy. Let self-love be your habit. The more you are willing to see the light, the more light will be seen. You are allowed to look for the light, reach for the light, and keep the light.

Remember the bad days are just temporary, you'll be okay. It's okay to do things to help you survive the bad days, too.

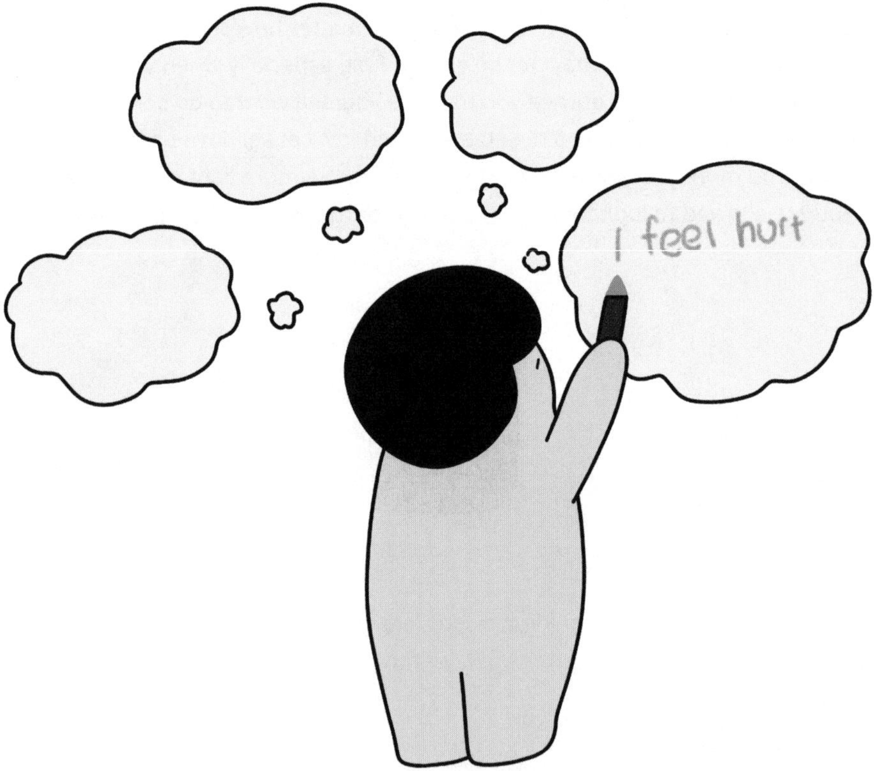
I feel hurt

write down how you really feel
let your feelings out of your mind

STAY HYDRATED

this can improve your mood

GET SOME SUNLIGHT
and exercise
your mood will be enhanced

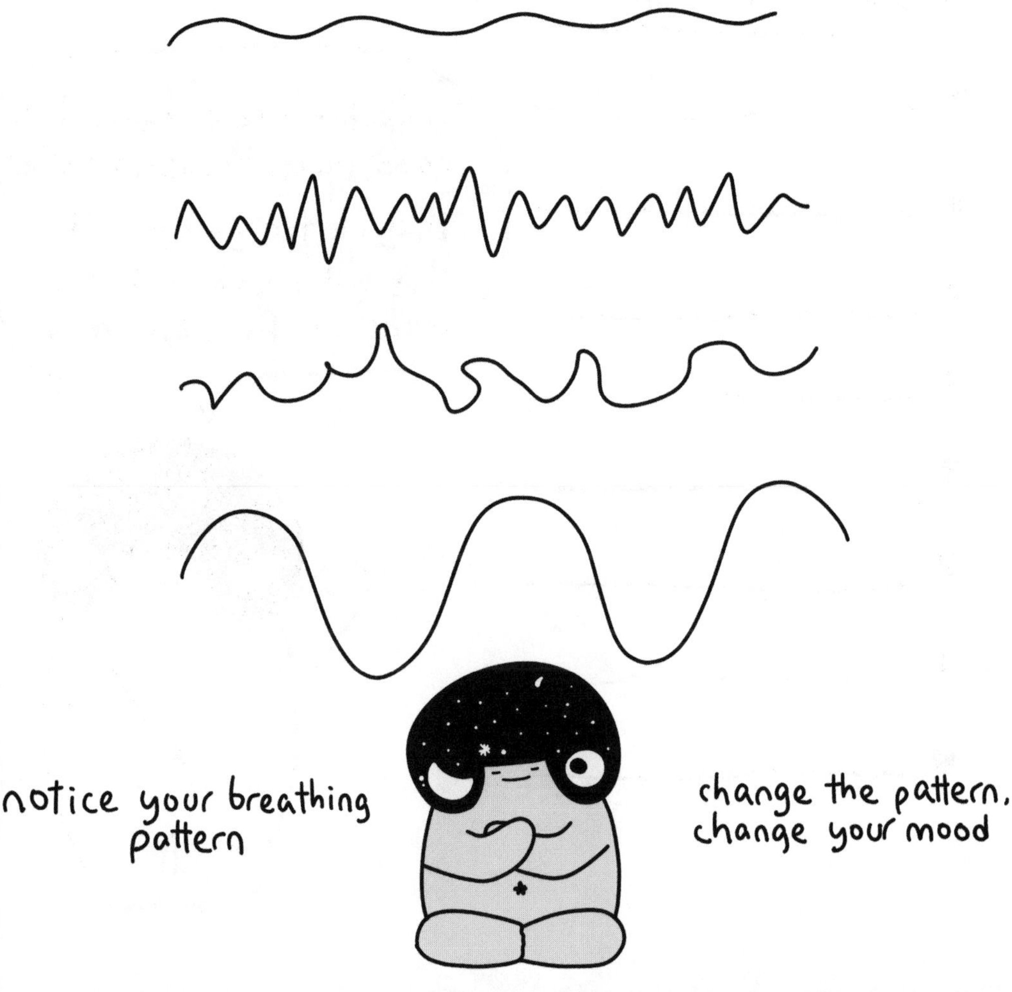
notice your breathing pattern
change the pattern, change your mood

GOOD THINGS IN LIFE

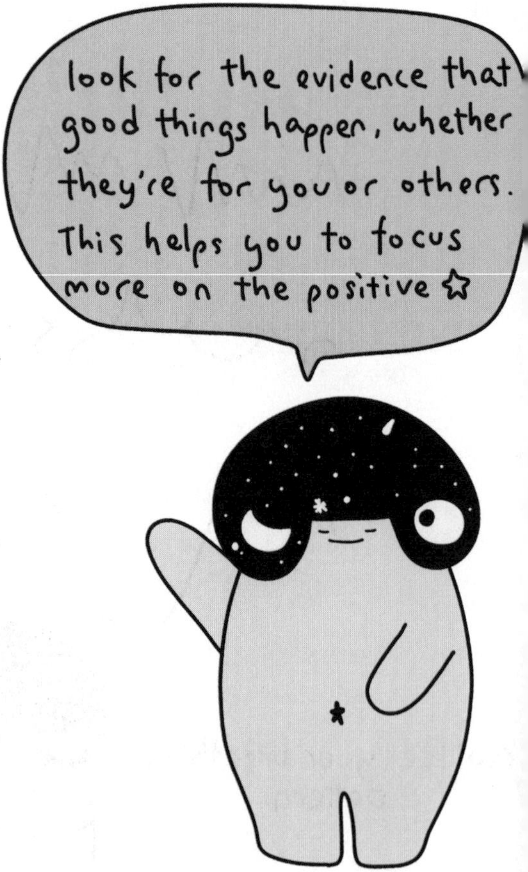

CHAPTER TWO

THERE IS ALWAYS A WAY OUT

-finding light in dark times to guide your way-

Finding Light in Dark Times to Guide Your Way

I want to go somewhere. I am not sure of the exact route to get there, but I've been looking for the signs for a long time. With the greatest hope that I will finally reach my destination this time, I enter a tunnel. It looks like a long one, "It's okay, it's just another challenge," I say to myself. As I walk, all of a sudden, darkness swallows me. I can't see which way to go, can't even locate where I am. What should I do? How do I get out of here? I keep searching for a way out, but there's no luck. I sit down on the cold floor, wondering if I will be stuck like this the rest of my life.

This is what I envision when I feel trapped.

When we get stuck, it seems to make no difference how hard we try, it feels there's simply no way out. And the scariest part is, this eventually becomes our belief—feeling that no matter what we do, the result will be the same. Then, we end up where we started, agree to live with it, but pity ourselves. If someone is kind enough to offer help, maybe we will try to convince them that this is our fate and nothing can be changed. We are trapped, and don't know what to expect other than the endless darkness.

The story doesn't have to end this way.

Regardless of where you are now—just entering the tunnel, having tried hard for a long time to find a way out, or desperately sitting on the floor—I am telling you, there is always a way out, and you will create a wonderful ending to this story. Because this is *your* story—you can write beautiful chapters.

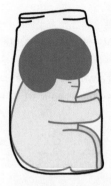

you'll be trapped here forever

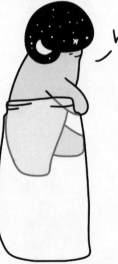

hehe, I won't

don't believe the words
that are not helping,
there's always a way out

if you feel like you are going around and around in circles
it's time to make a move and do something different

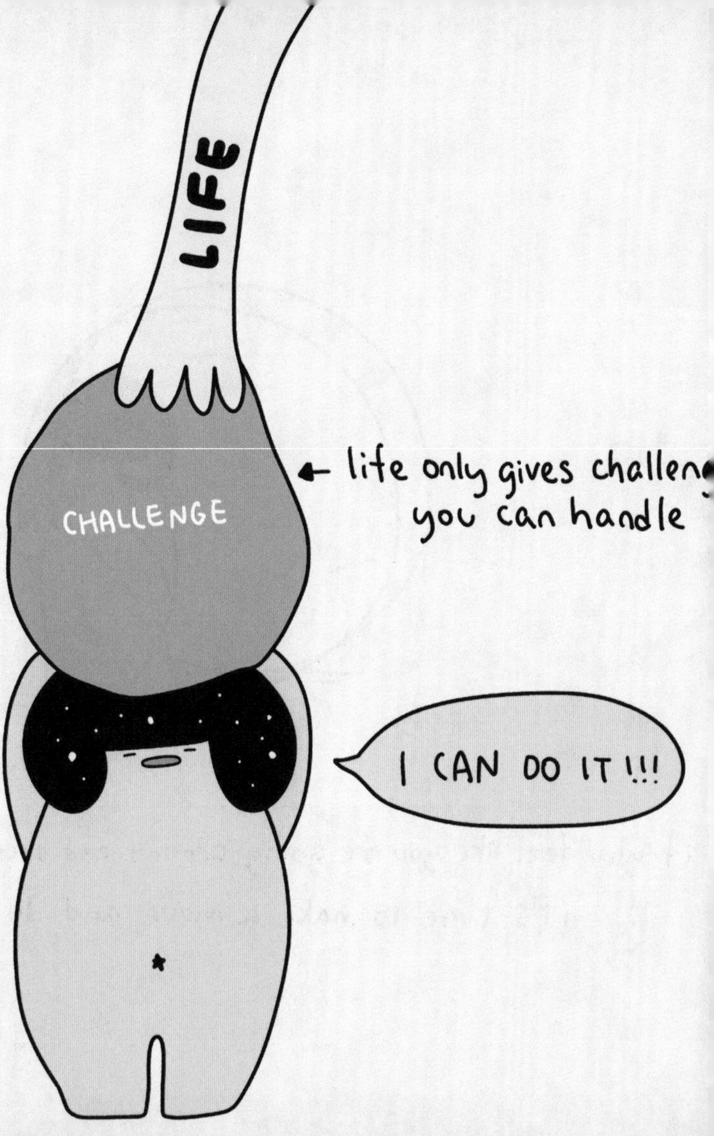
LIFE
CHALLENGE
life only gives challeng
you can handle
I CAN DO IT!!!

it makes you feel worse
if you keep looking at what's done

let's focus on how to
make things better

When I feel trapped, I usually find myself facing two scenarios. Either I think I have no choice, or that I have done everything but still can't get what I want. While the feelings are valid, isn't it still possible to get unstuck?

First things first, we always have a choice—something we must always remember. We make many decisions everyday, from activities of daily living, to big decisions that might change the course of our life. We list out the choices in our head before we make decisions. "Which one is better?" "What consequence will it bring?" "How do I feel about that?" Some decisions can be made easily, some not, especially those which create misalignment for our heart and mind.

When our mind sends us a message on what we should do, but our heart knows that it isn't for us, this is where the stress comes in. The mind message is sometimes too strong and becomes our obligation. When we refuse to do it, guilt and shame might strike our heart. That's why we decide the mind message is the only option. It means we have no choice, doesn't it? So we do what we *should* do, thinking we are doing the right thing, but knowing we are not happy. Who would be happy to do something unwillingly?

Most of the time when we feel we have no choice, it's not because there is just one single option, but because we screen out all the other options. We choose what we should do, sometimes because of our loved ones, societal norms, our past, or other reasons. No matter what it is, the end result is that we choose what we think is "best" for us at the moment.

"What if I don't like that choice?"

If you hear this question inside of you, choose again. Even if there's a concrete reason for you to pick one option, you are not probably happy. People often measure their success by others' expectations or society norms, like being rich, getting married, having kids, getting fit...To me, the only measurement in life now is how joyful I am, and how much kindness I can spread. Your happiness matters!

"If I had a better option, I wouldn't feel trapped. I want something else!" you may say. I have thought this many, many times, and I can almost hear my heart's response:

THINK AGAIN!
what do you REALLY want?

I was shocked the first time I heard this question, and surprisingly, that I could give a different answer.

what I REALLY want

← what I think I want

"What I want" and "what I really want" are often two different things, but they are connected. "What I really want" is where your hidden emotions and higher purpose are. Like when someone says they want a wonderful relationship, what they really want could to be loved and cherished by another; when someone says they want to be rich, what they really want perhaps is to be free and enjoy life, or to provide a better home for their family. When we focus on the "what I really want," it is possible for us to see more options to achieve a better outcome.

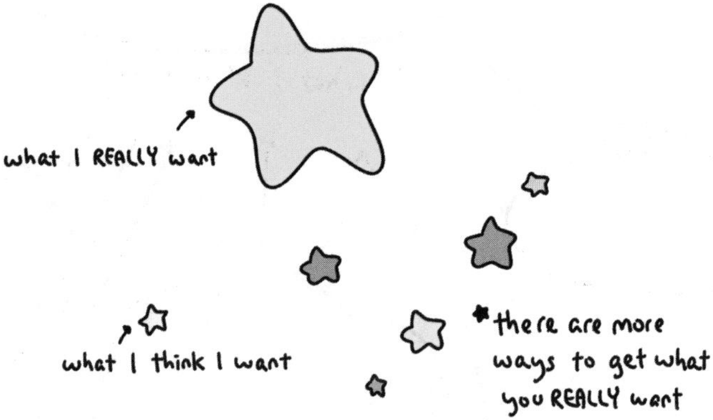
what I REALLY want
what I think I want
*there are more ways to get what you REALLY want

Once we realize that we *do* have choices, we are free to explore and experience.

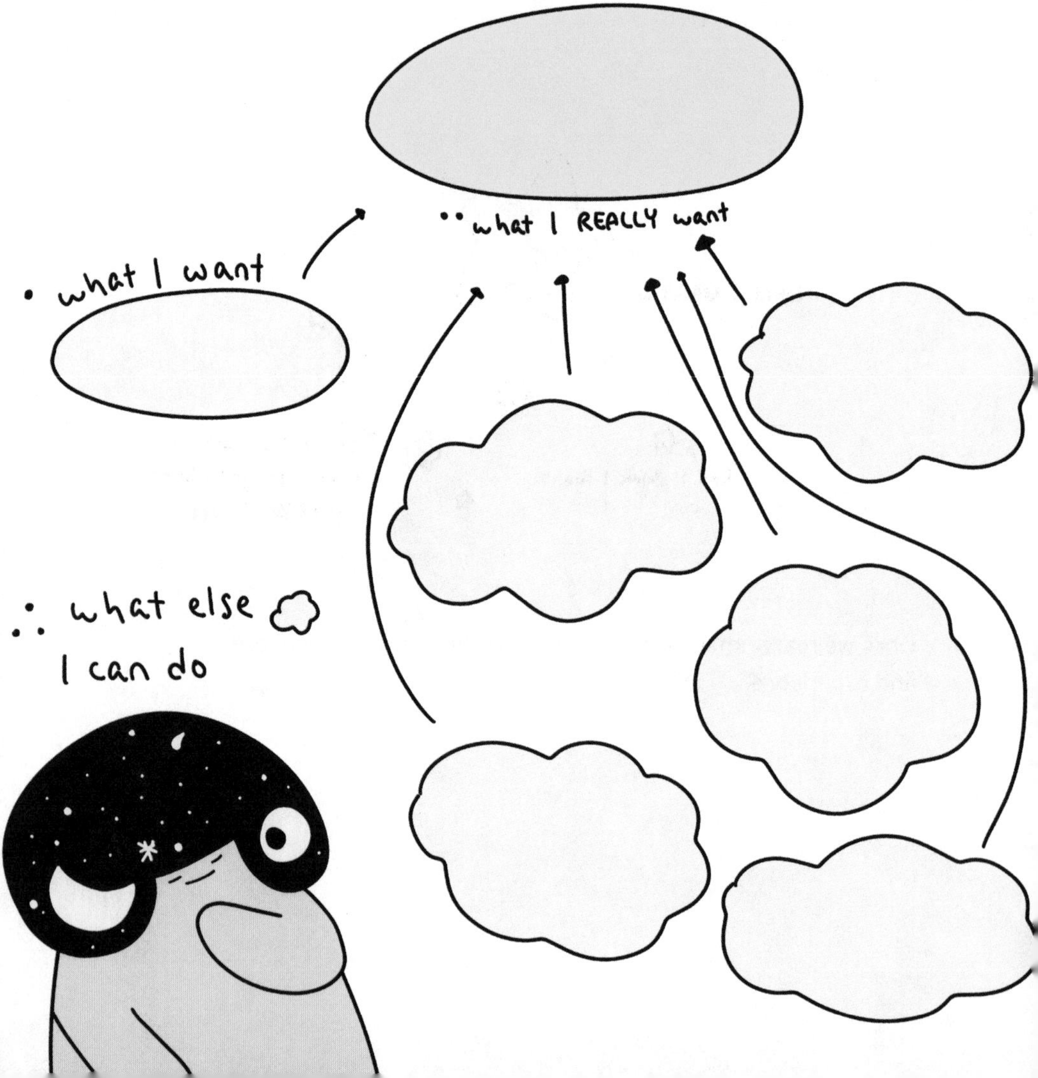
• what I want
•• what I REALLY want
∴ what else
I can do

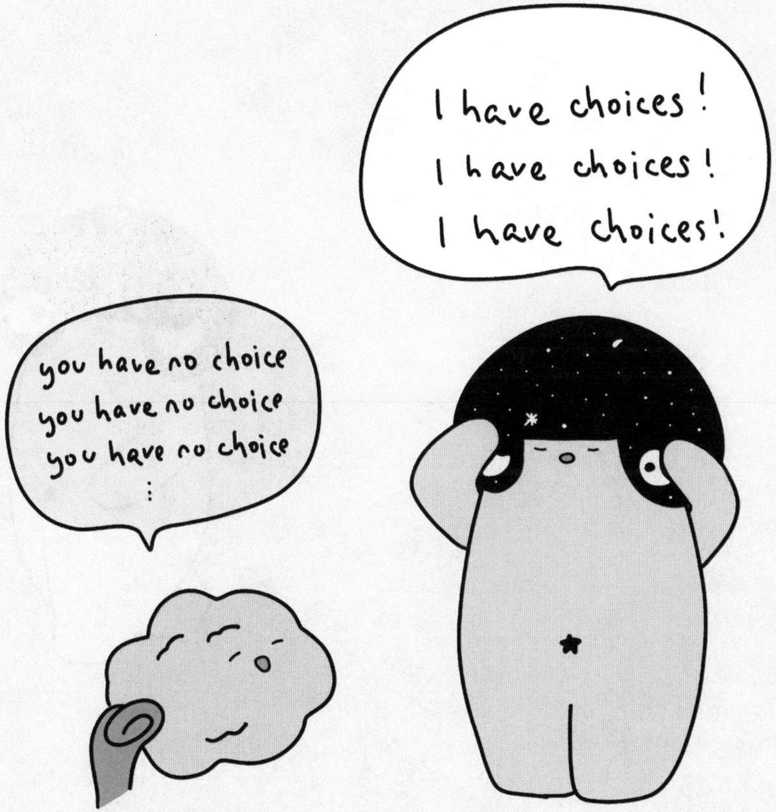
I have choices!
I have choices!
I have choices!
you have no choice
you have no choice
you have no choice
⋮

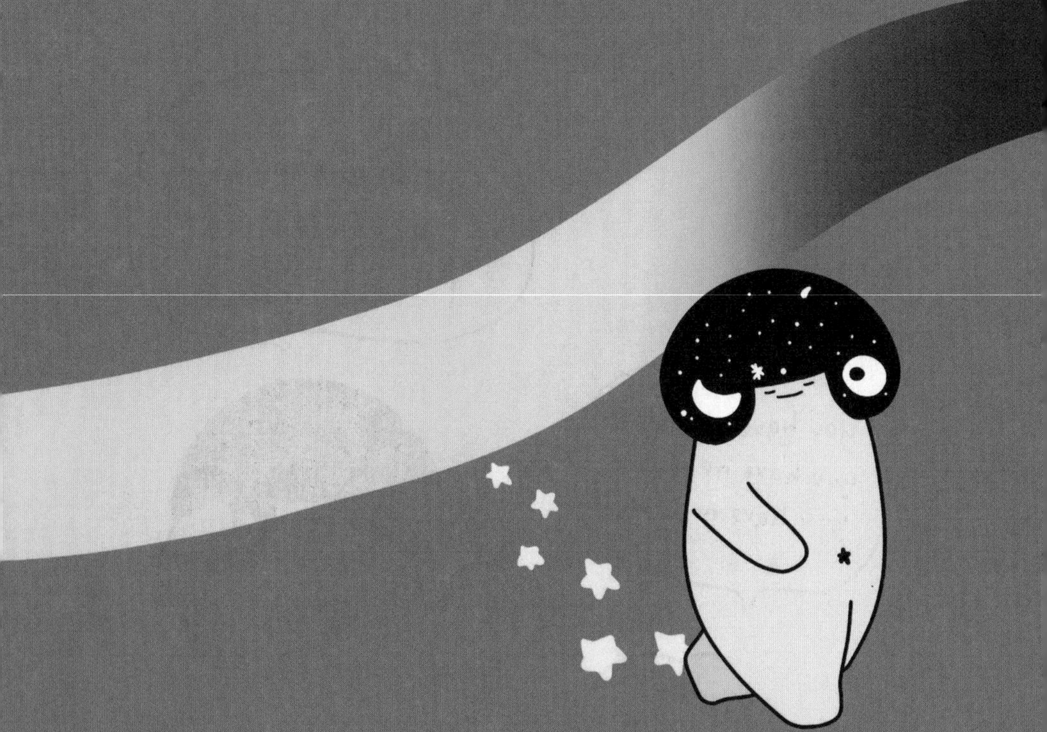

If the original plan isn't leading you
to somewhere nice, it's okay to change your plan

there are things you can control
and there are things you can't

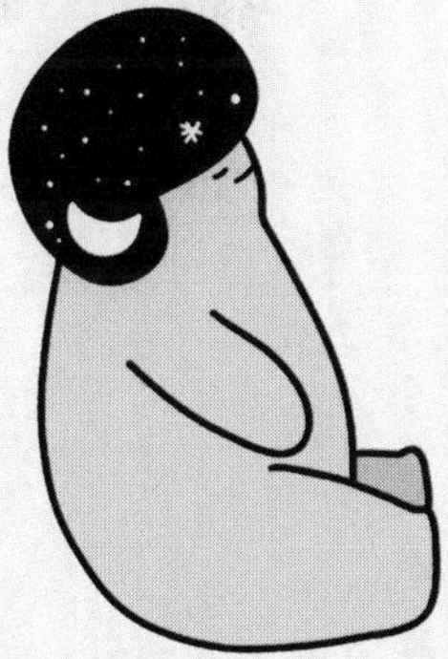

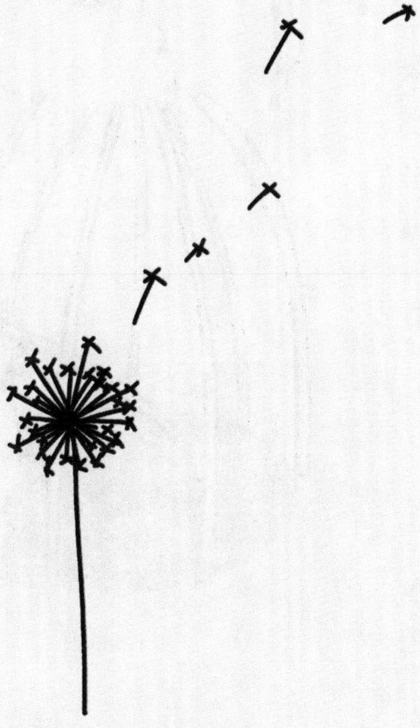

let go of those you can't control

I should...
I can't ...
I never used to ...

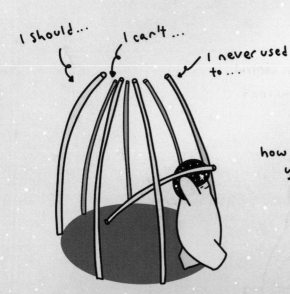

look at
how many bars you use to restrict yourself from being free

YOU CAN REMOVE THEM
IF YOU WANT TO

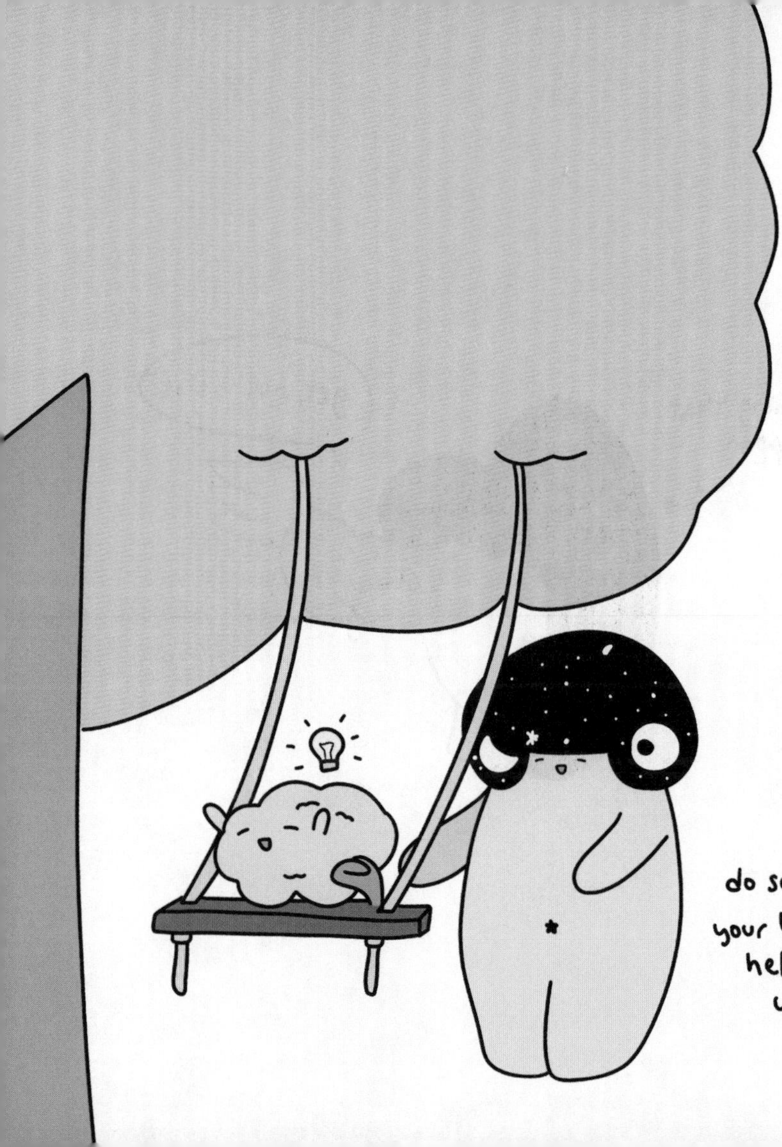

do something to distract your busy mind, it may help you to come up with new ideas

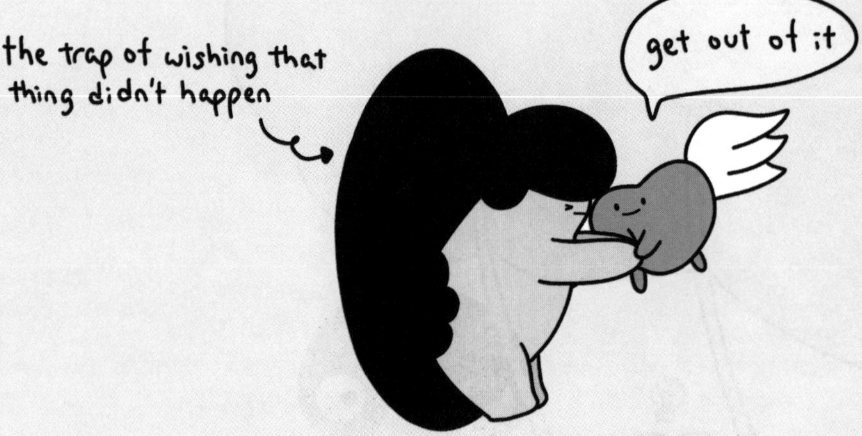
the trap of wishing that thing didn't happen
get out of it

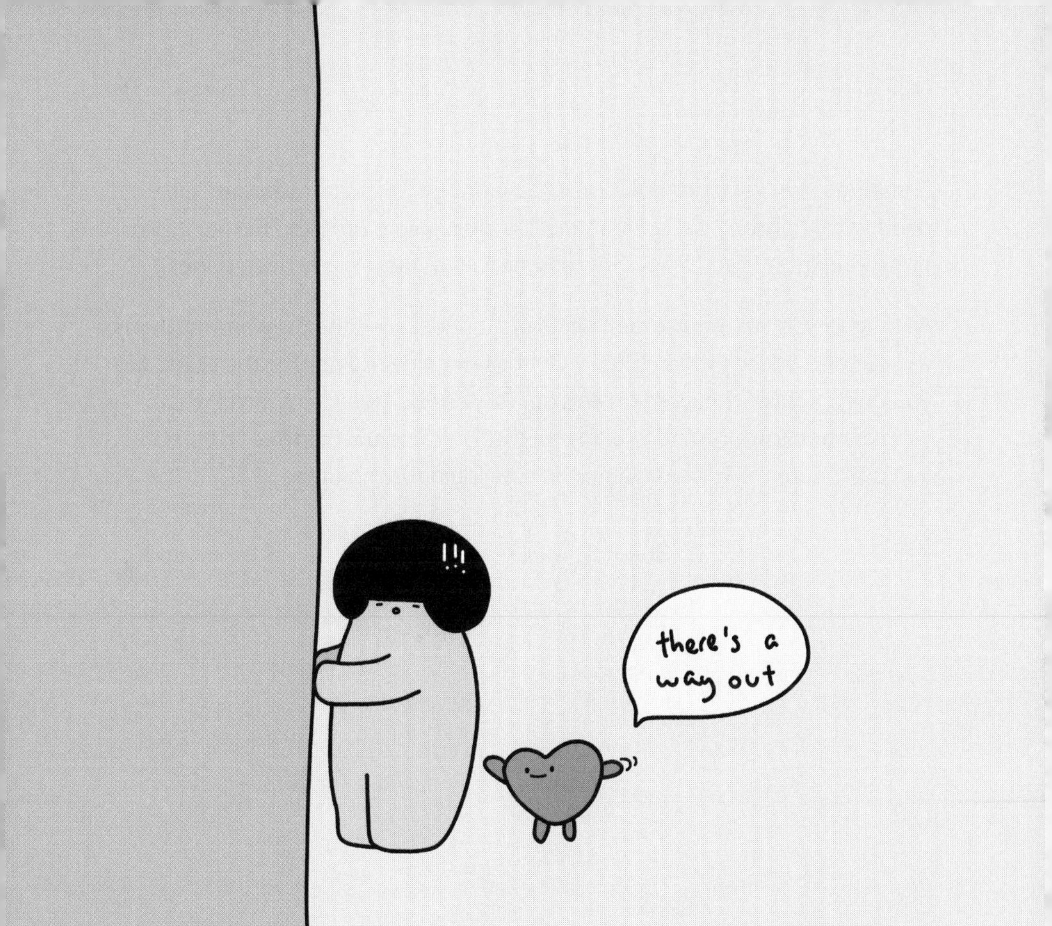
there's a way out

your heart knows what to do
you just need to listen to what it says

Sometimes we get stuck because we are not getting what we want. "Do I need to try harder?" we wonder, or, "Do I just give it up?" The former is so tiring, the latter is so disappointing, when a lot has already been done.

As long as you still want it, don't give up. Just because the previous methods didn't work, doesn't mean the project has to be over. Look for the clues. Are you doing similar things again and again? Are you trying to control what you cannot control? Are there any methods that you would like to try but you don't dare to? Is there someone you could reach out to?

sometimes fear makes you feel stuck

but you have the courage to get through that

HAVE FAITH IN YOURSELF

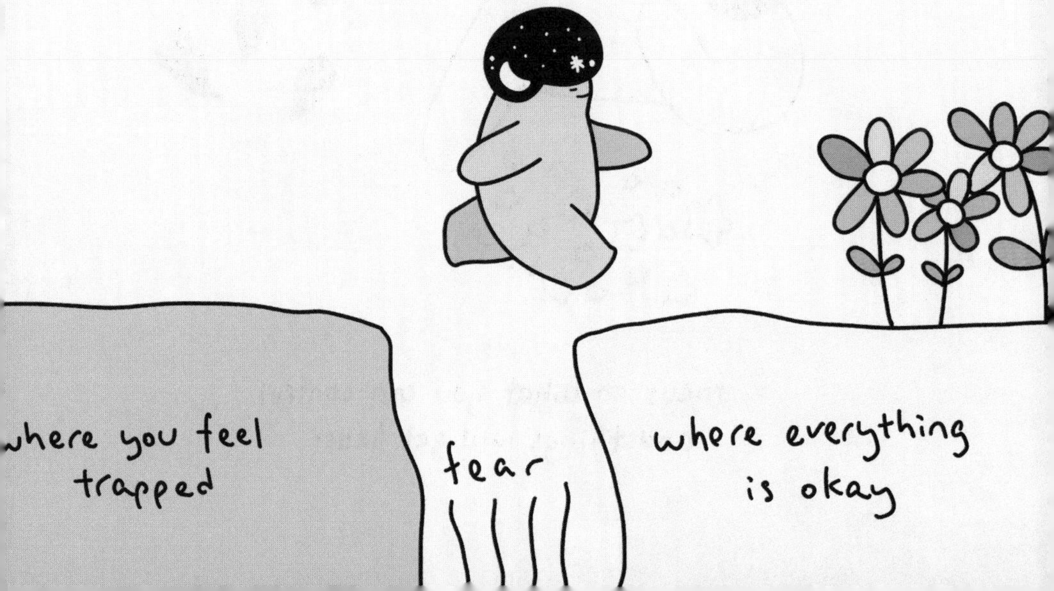
where you feel trapped
fear
where everything is okay

focus on what you can control
and things will get better

sometimes you forget the stars you have

≷you can do it≷

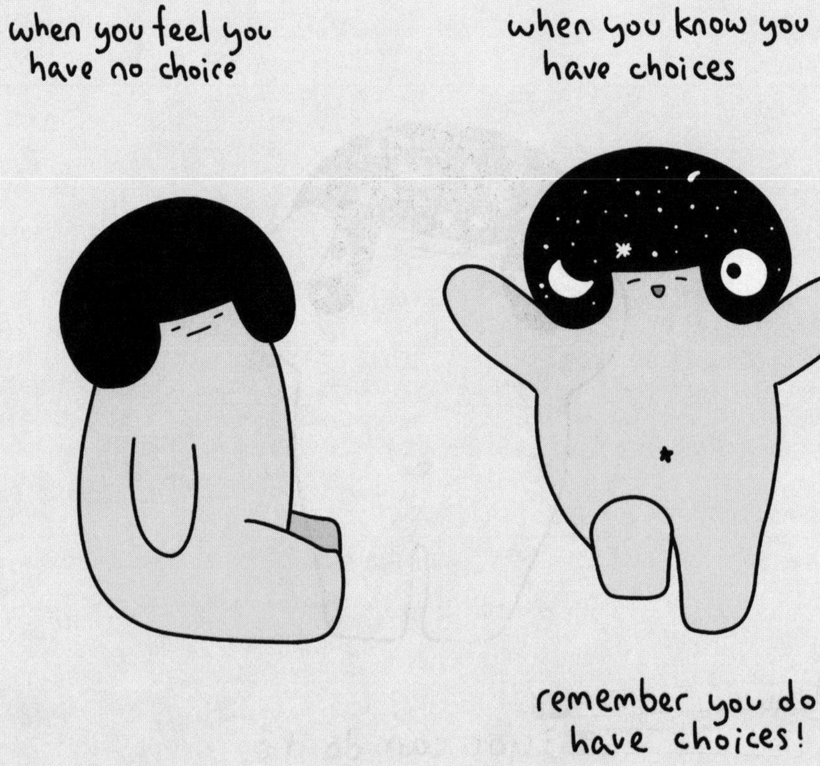
when you feel you have no choice
when you know you have choices
remember you do have choices!

may you choose to make love-based decisions

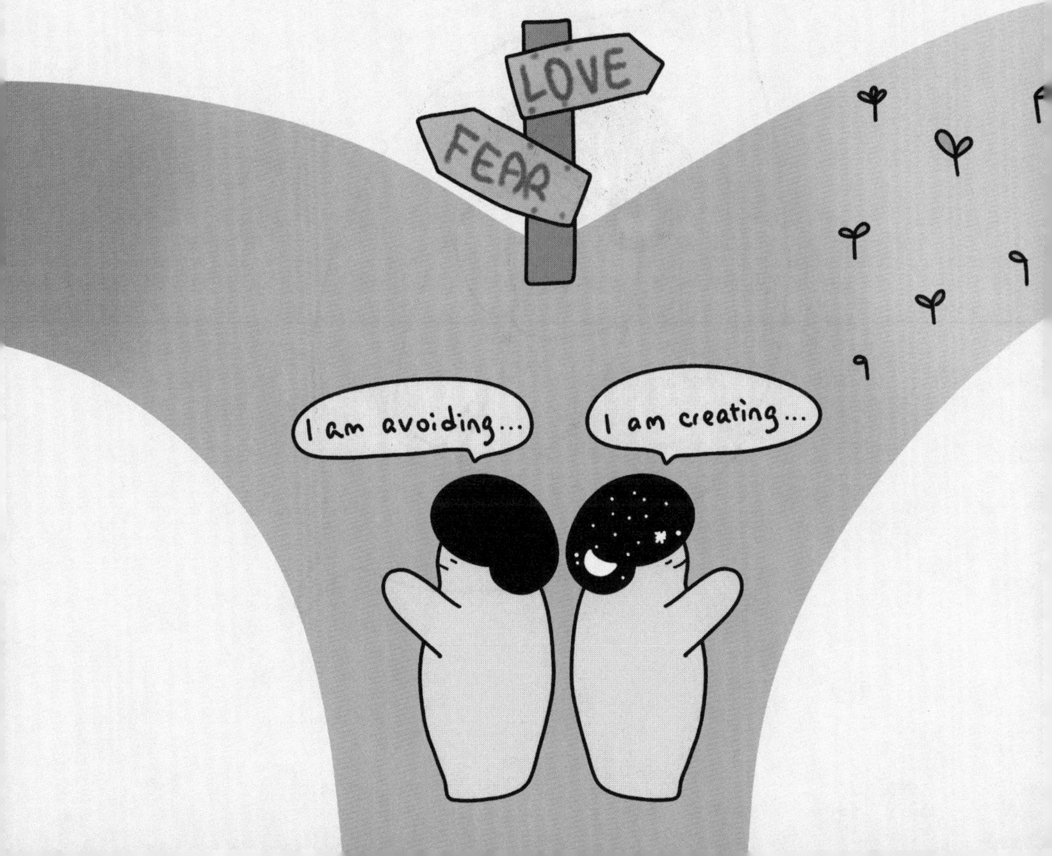
LOVE
FEAR
I am avoiding...
I am creating...

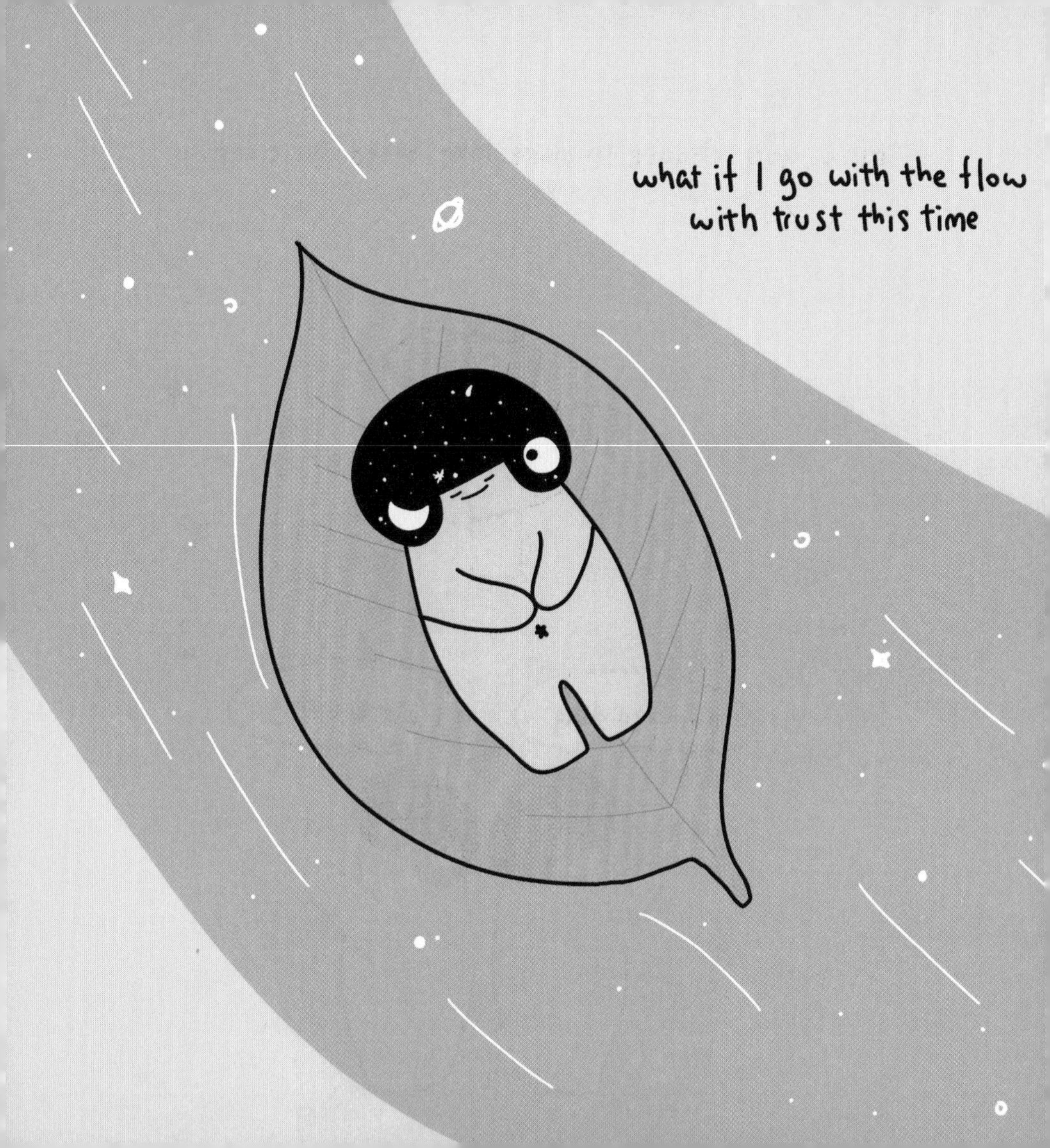
what if I go with the flow
with trust this time

it's okay to put down your
busy mind for a while

sometimes you just grow so much that the same thing
doesn't serve you any more
it's okay to get unstuck!!

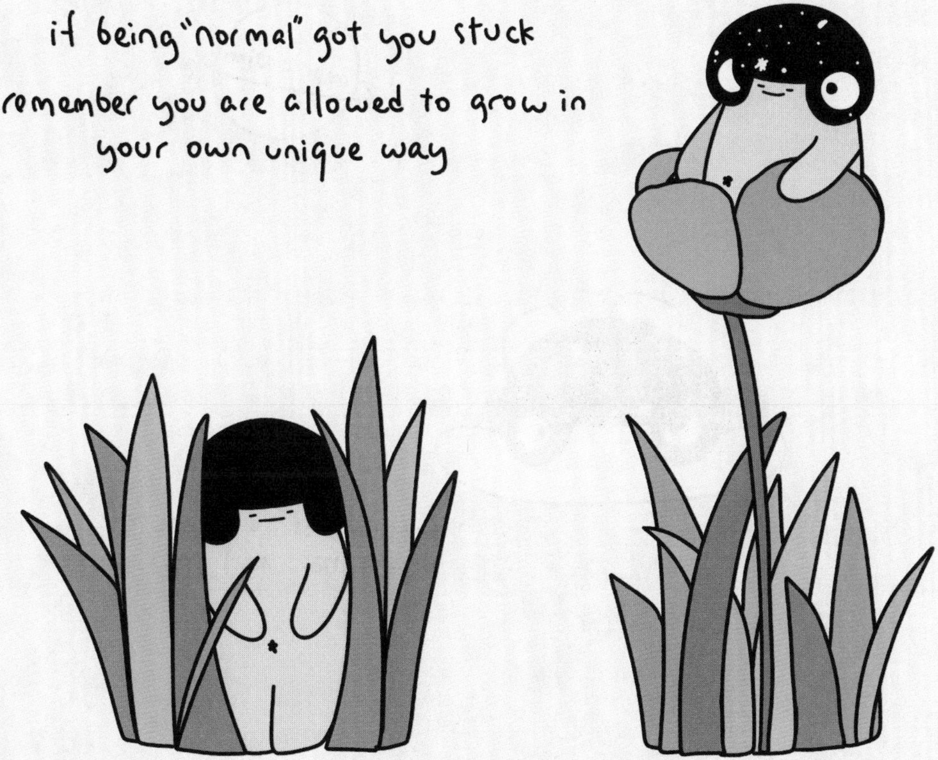
if being "normal" got you stuck
remember you are allowed to grow in
your own unique way

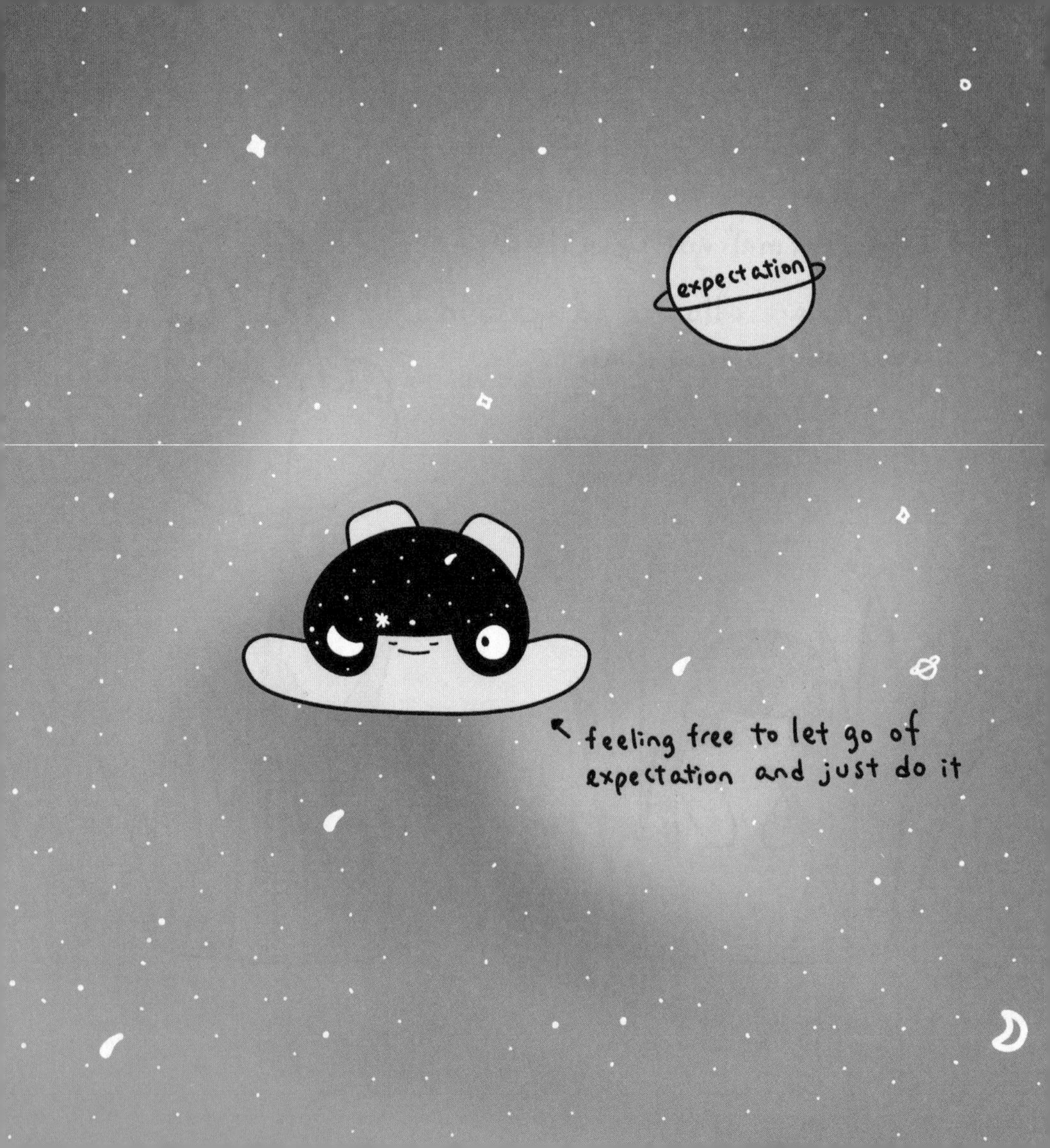
expectation
feeling free to let go of expectation and just do it

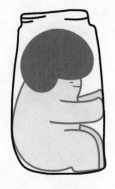

you'll be trapped here forever

hehe, I won't

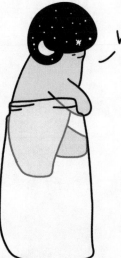

don't believe the words that are not helping, there's always a way out

remember the reason why you
wanted to do something,
let this be the fuel that keep
you moving

your intention

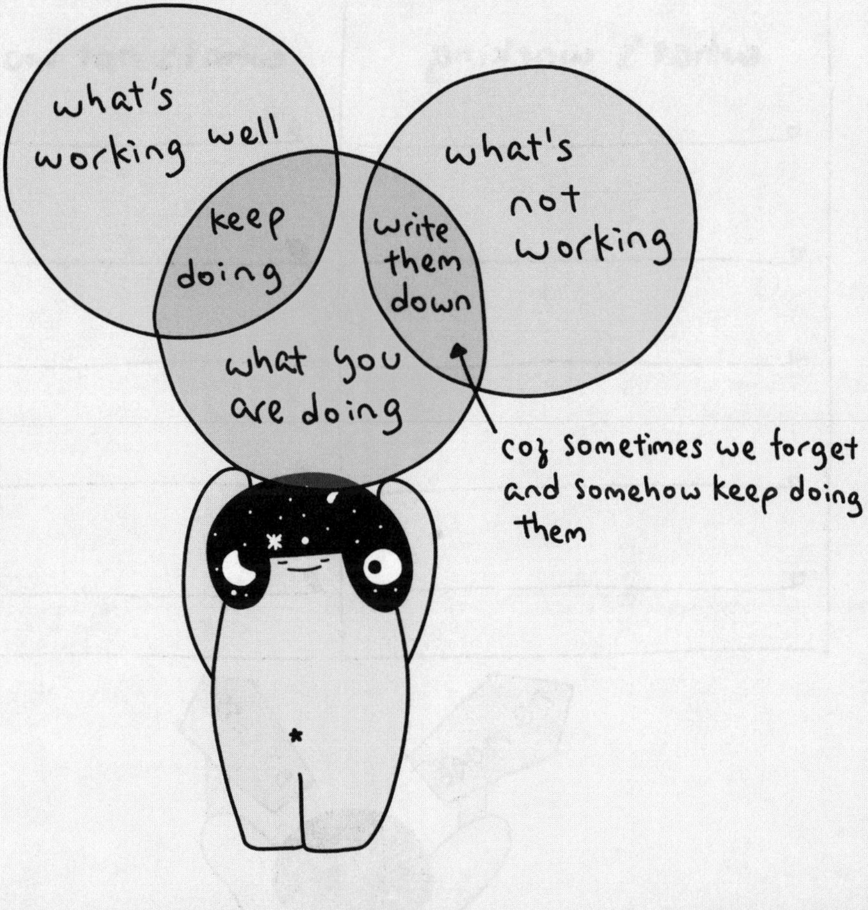
what's working well
what's not working
keep doing
write them down
what you are doing
coz sometimes we forget and somehow keep doing them

what's working	what's not working

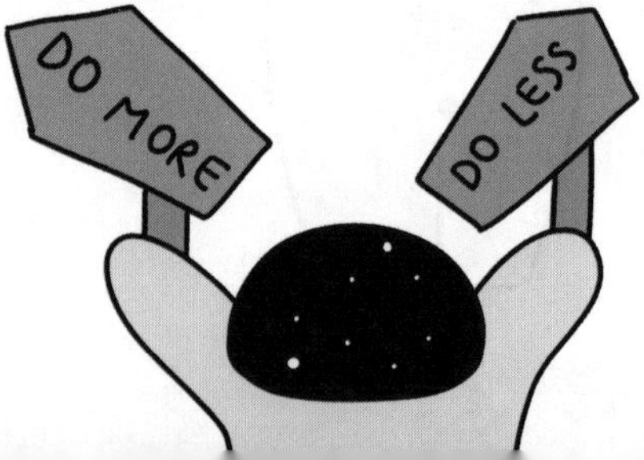
DO MORE
DO LESS

There are a few questions you can ask yourself if you feel trapped again in the future:

> Is this a SHOULD do instead of a "really want" to do?

> Am I doing this out of love or fear?

> Is it that I can't do it? Or that I don't want to do it at all?

> What's the worst case scenario if I was not doing this?

> Would I still do this if no one was watching me?

> If I were free to do anything with all the resources I needed, and no one to judge me, what would I do?

By answering these self-reflection questions, you will realize where you were heading before and where you would like to go now. There is no right or wrong answer, just the hints as to why you are feeling trapped. Here is one last question to ask yourself:

> Am I willing to take back control of my life?

CHAPTER THREE

I AM WORTHY ; I WAS BORN WORTHY

-learning to see your worth-

Learning to See Your Worth

Whether you know how to shine your light, or you have never felt you are enough, there are always moments when we doubt our worthiness. "Why do I make the same mistake over and over again?" "Why am I still crying every day, even though he left a year ago?" "Why am I not feeling better even though I go to therapy once a week?" "Why can everyone do that but I can't?" These questions circle around in our mind. And then, we think, "I am so useless, I need help." Once the negative thought spiral begins, it's an easy task to create even more messages like these. But what you focus on determines your destiny. Do you want a bright one or a dark one?

I am sure you have heard the phrase "practice makes progress". When you keep doing something for a period of time, you will definitely sharpen the skill. If you constantly judge yourself, you are actually training your brain to see only the negative parts of yourself. Once this autopilot mode is set, you will feel like you don't have goodness and potential inside of you. The truth is, however, that there are stars in you, and you are just trained not to see them.

Here's the great news though—if we can train ourselves to see only the bad things, we can train ourselves to see the good things, too.

But how?

I once tried to say "I love you" in front of a mirror in order to gain some self-love. Fake it until you make it, right? But I felt so odd because, when I didn't actually believe what I said, I couldn't feel the love at all. Every time I did this, there was a battle inside of my head. Not only I was I *not* feeling the love, but it also made me further doubt my ability to love myself at all. It does work for some people, but sadly I am not one of them. If you are just like me, you may not find a positive effect by forcing yourself to say the pre-set positive affirmations. That's okay.

We are all unique, one affirmation doesn't fit us all. It's okay to make your own affirmations, to achieve the greatest results for yourself. A key to creating affirmations is to use only positive words.

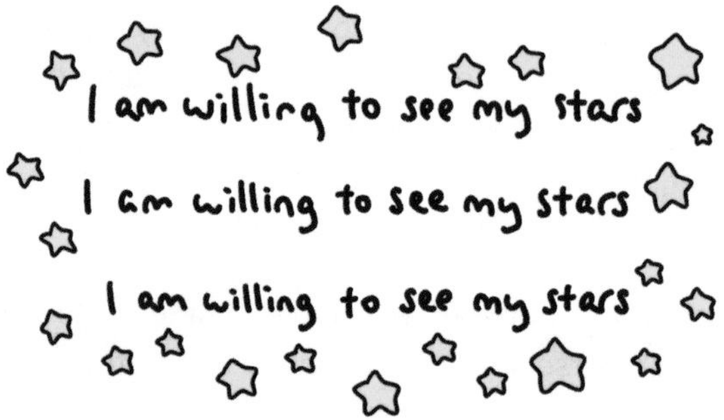
I am willing to see my stars
I am willing to see my stars
I am willing to see my stars

After you've made your own affirmations, read them to see if you feel good about them. When you feel positive, write them down on paper and post them in a noticeable place. Read them in the morning, and before you go to bed. Feel the good vibes in your body.

Now sit back and relax, and get ready to see your stars.

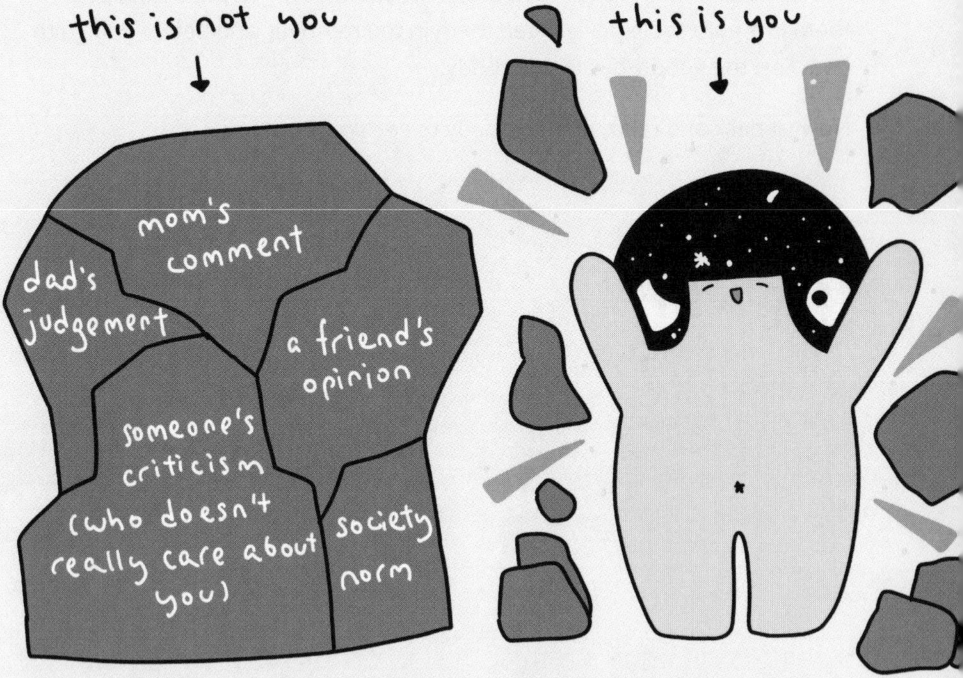
this is not you
this is you
mom's comment
dad's judgement
a friend's opinion
someone's criticism (who doesn't really care about you)
society norm

don't let those comments shape you
you are amazing just the way you are

PERFECT

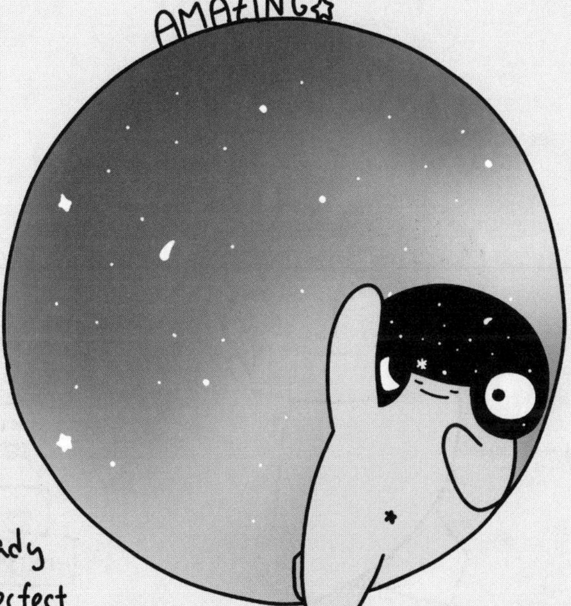
AMAZING

being you is amazing already
you don't need to be perfect

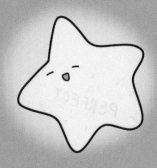

everyone makes mistakes

may you use them to reach your stars

mistake
mistake mistake
mistake mistake mistake
mistake mistake
mistake mistake
mistake mistake mistake
MISTAKE
mistake mistake mistake
mistake mistake mistake

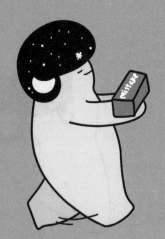

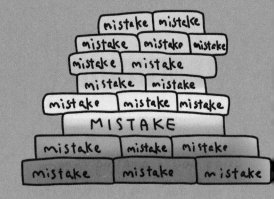

you don't need to compare yourself with others

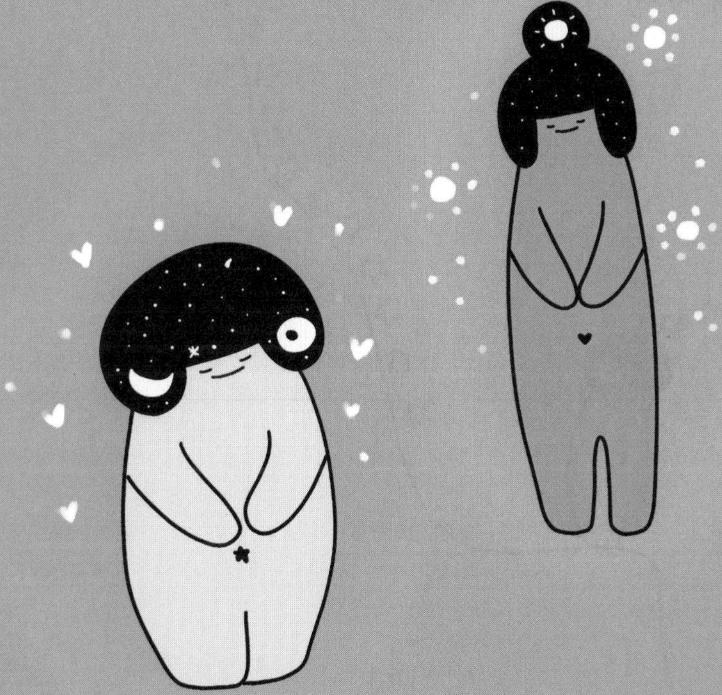

we all shine in our own way

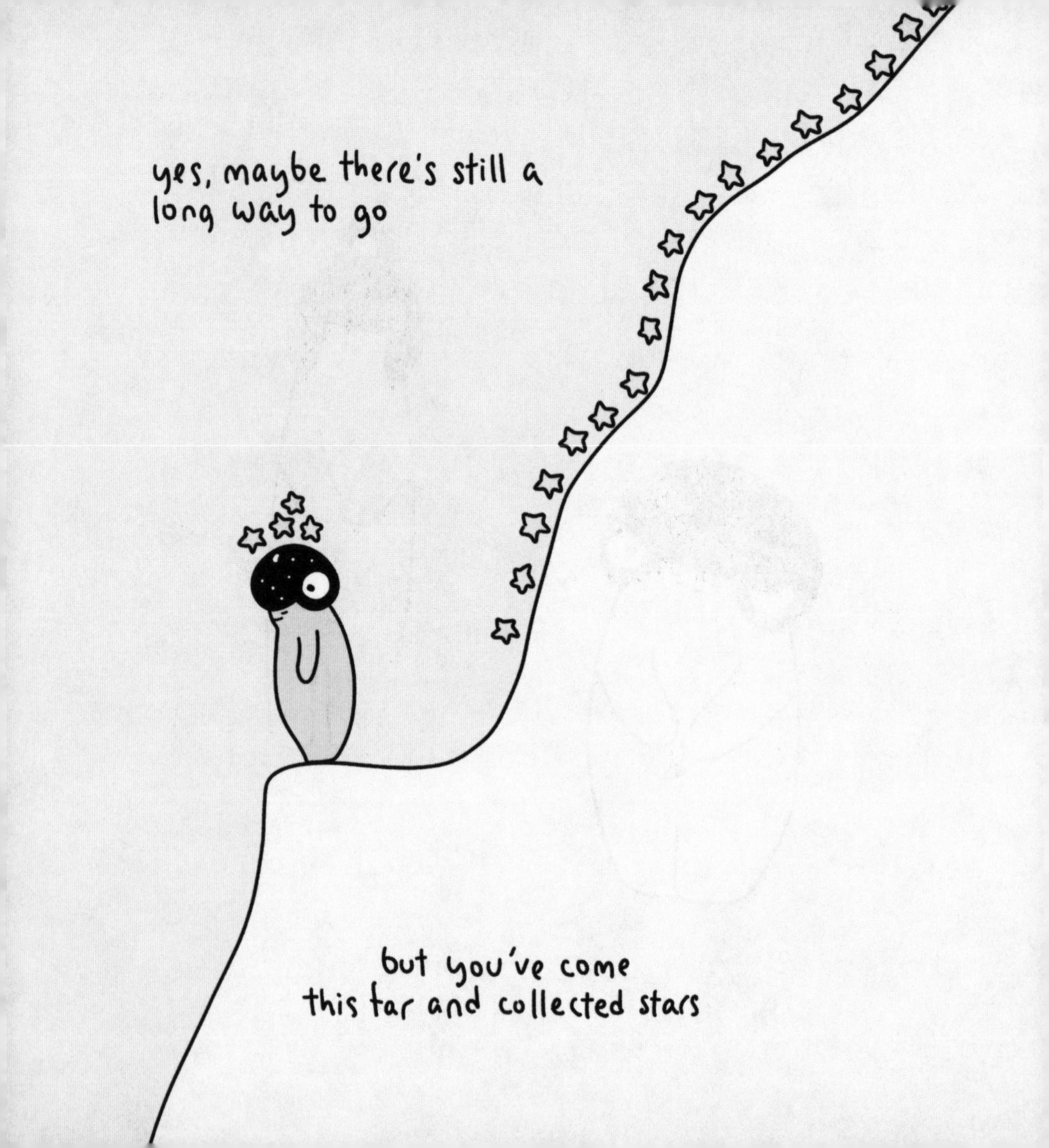
yes, maybe there's still a long way to go
but you've come this far and collected stars

just because some people can't see your stars
doesn't mean you have no star

you can't be happy if you keep counting how many mistakes you've made
yeah, I've made it this far
celebrate how far you've come

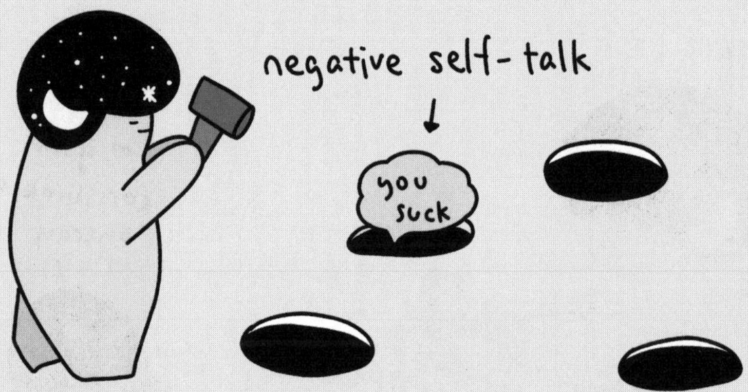
negative self-talk
you suck

hey dear, be kind to yourself

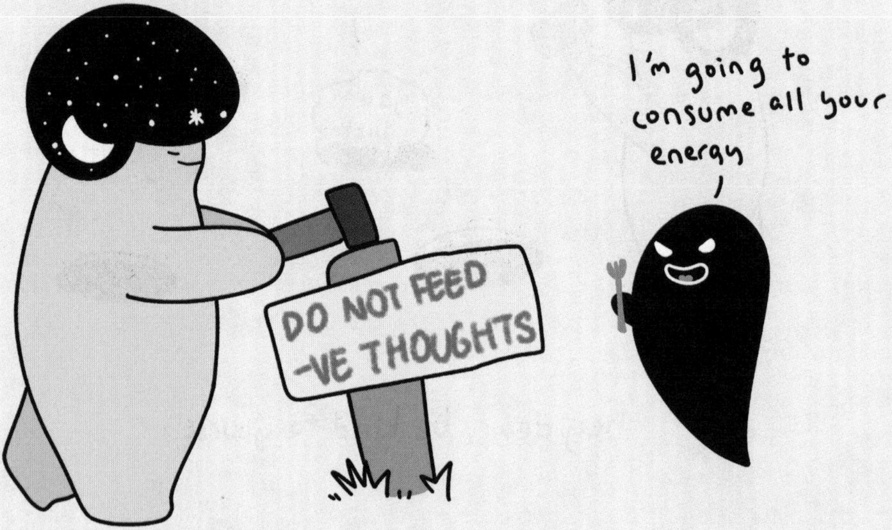
DO NOT FEED
-VE THOUGHTS
I'm going to consume all your energy

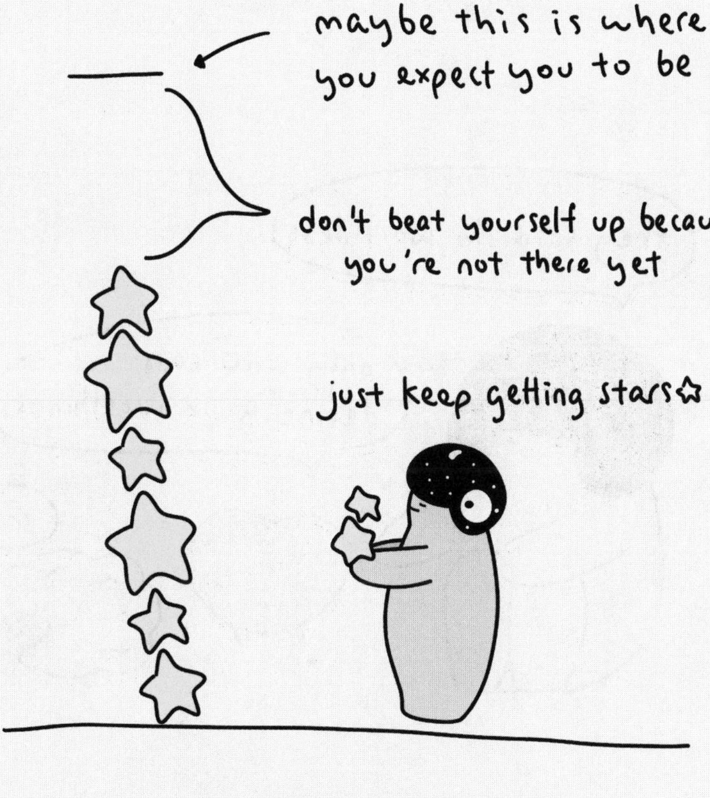
maybe this is where you expect you to be
don't beat yourself up because you're not there yet
just keep getting stars

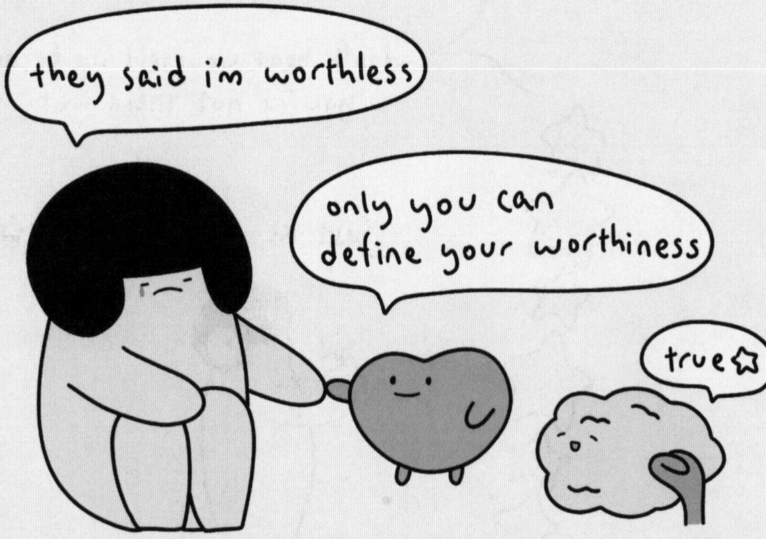
they said i'm worthless
only you can define your worthiness
true

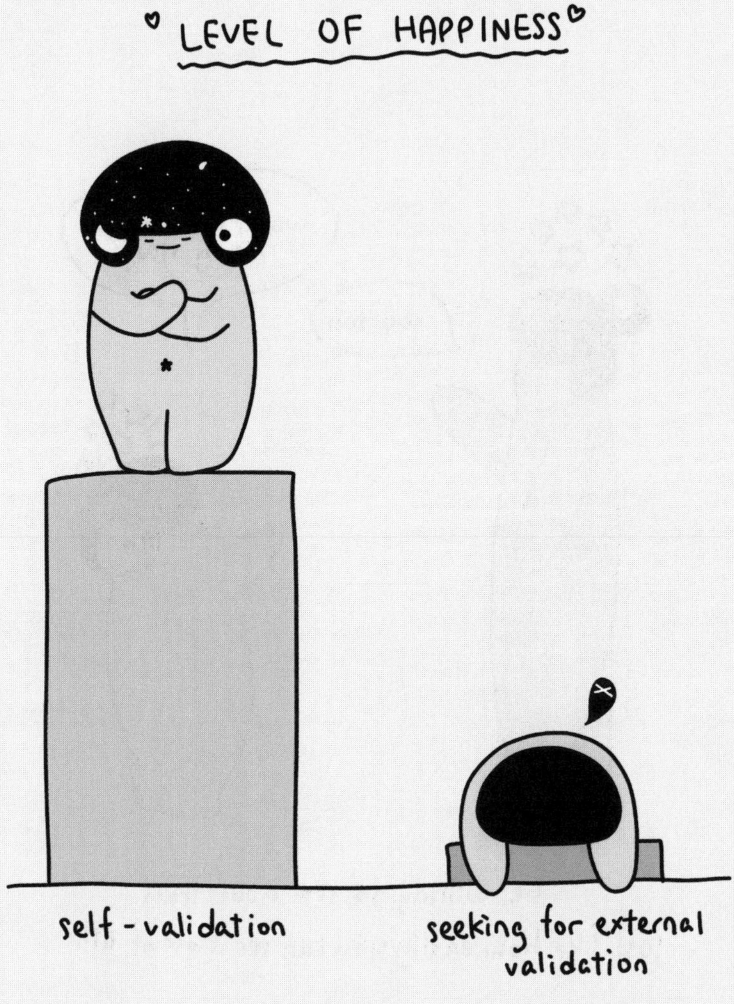
LEVEL OF HAPPINESS
self-validation
seeking for external validation

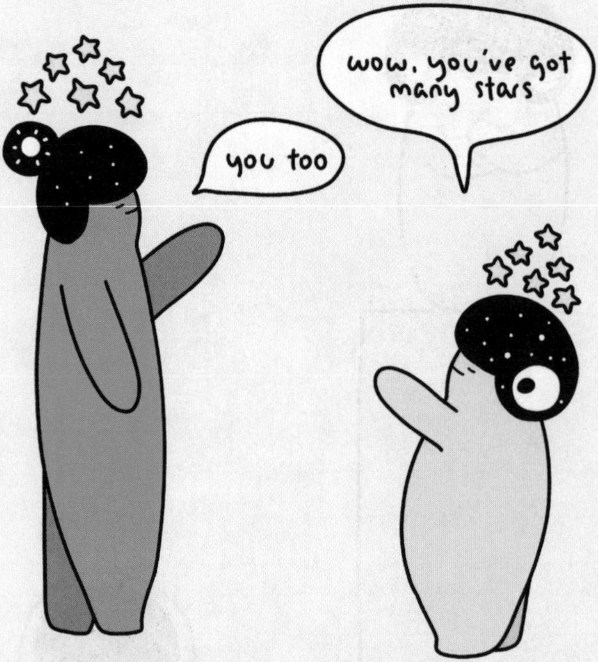
wow, you've got many stars
you too

be willing to see your stars
just like how easily you can see those of others

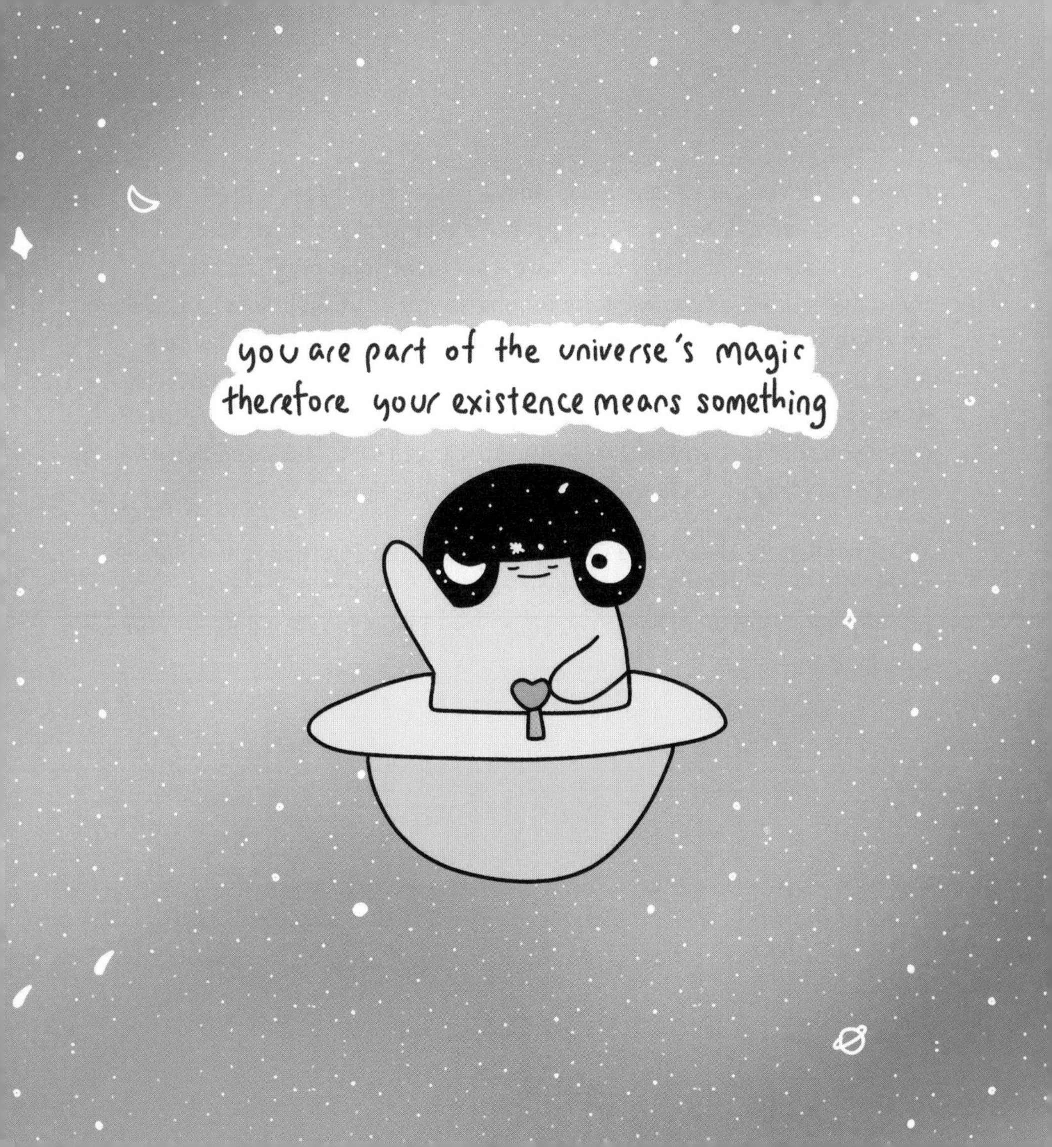
you are part of the universe's magic
therefore your existence means something

If you feel like you are a failure, let me ask you—what is failure? Failure is when we do something, and don't get the result we want, right? Well, most of your endeavors probably don't have a set timeframe, meaning you can try as many times as you want, for as long as you want. So unless you give up, there's always a chance to get what you want. Your so-called failure is just a part of the journey to success. You may not have gotten what you want *yet*, but you are definitely not a failure. If there are people that have called you so, I am sorry for them—they projected their unwanted negative emotions onto you. It's not your problem, you are fine.

You are fine because you tried, you showed up, and you took action. Maybe you've tried so many times that you've started to believe you're a failure, but hey, your hard work earns you stars. Those little stars accumulate, and will shine one day.

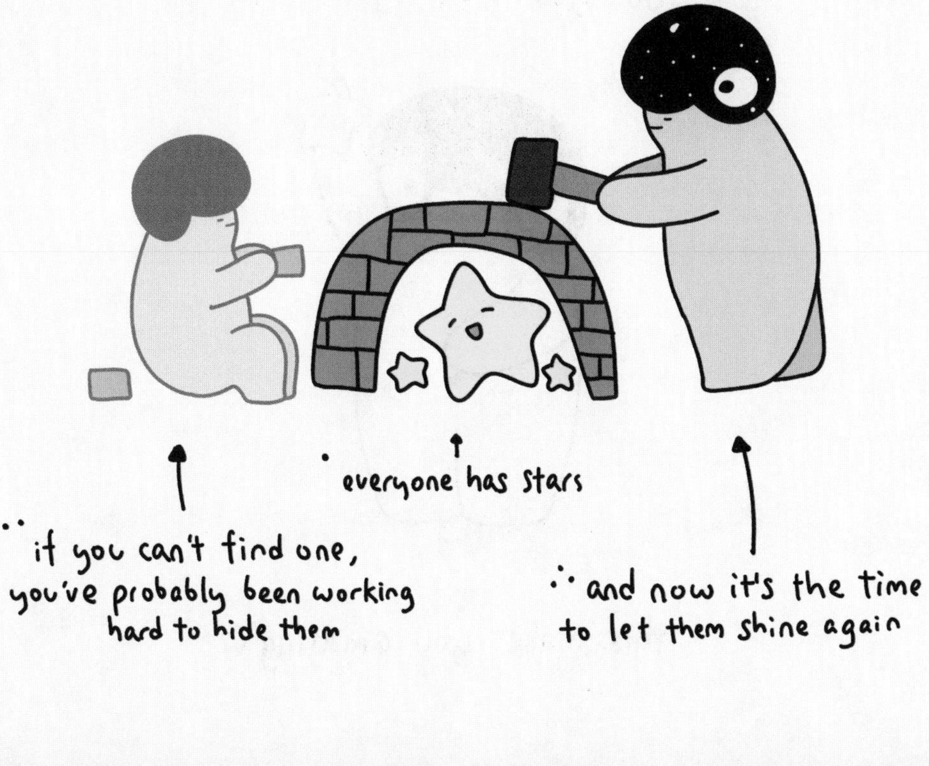
everyone has stars
if you can't find one, you've probably been working hard to hide them
and now it's the time to let them shine again

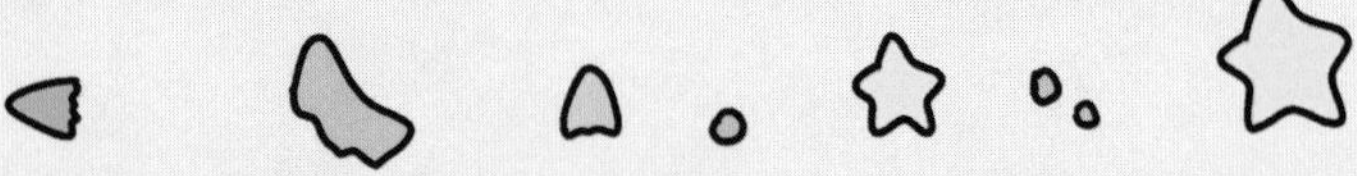

yes, you've made mistakes
but you've also got stars

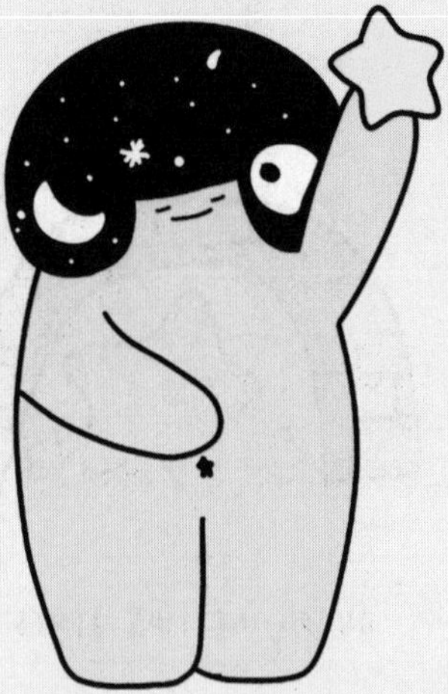

this makes you amazing ☆

maybe there are things
you're not proud of

fault
weakness
flaw
failure
past
mistakes

this is where you mine
your stars ☆

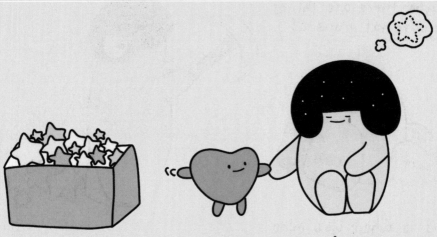

sometimes you just forget how
many stars you've collected

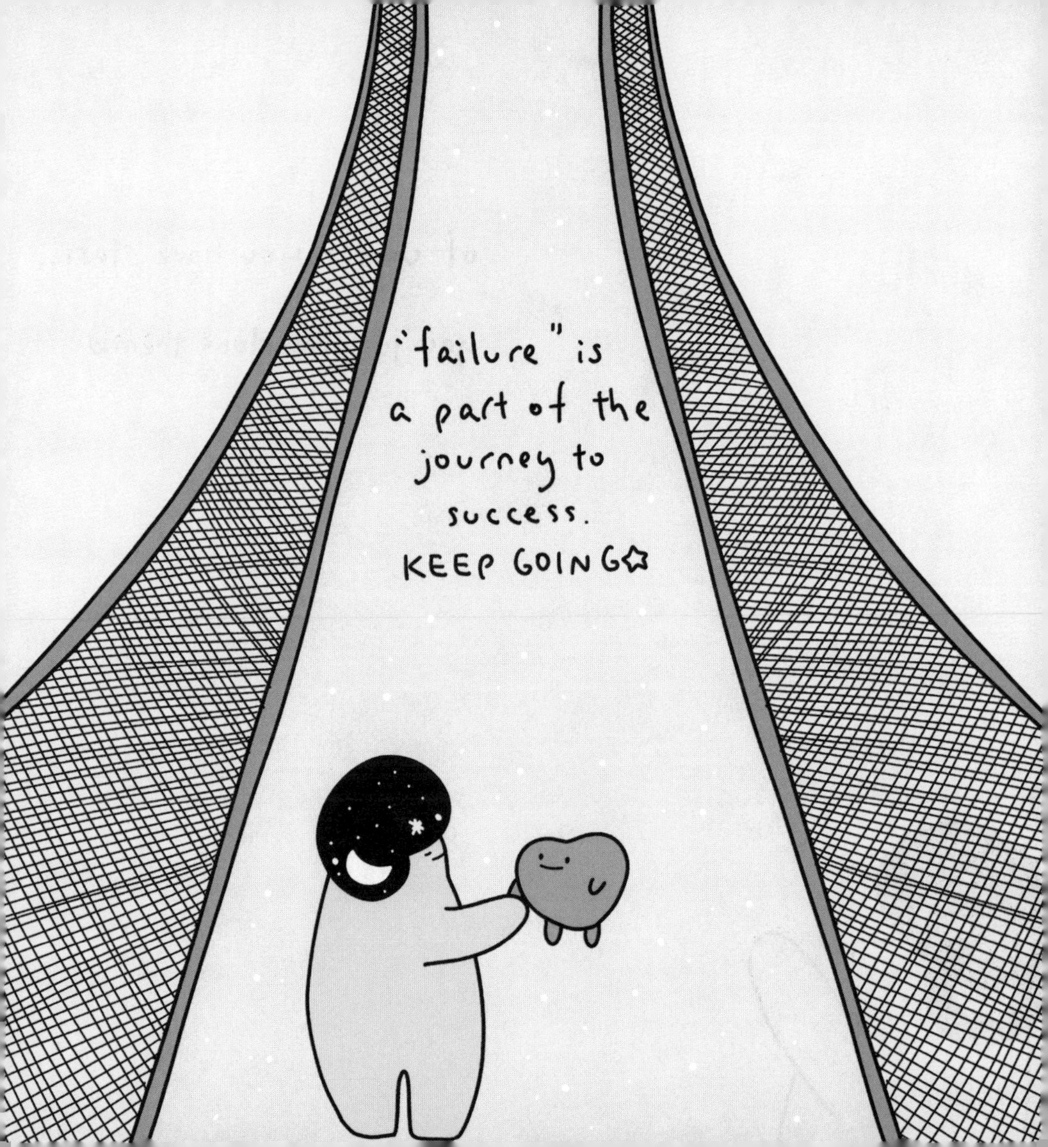
"failure" is
a part of the
journey to
success.
KEEP GOING

of course you have stars,

you just overlook them♡

is my star too small?

when you compare yourself
with others

LOOK! this is my star

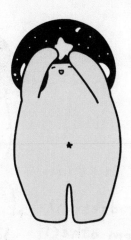

when you focus on
yourself♡

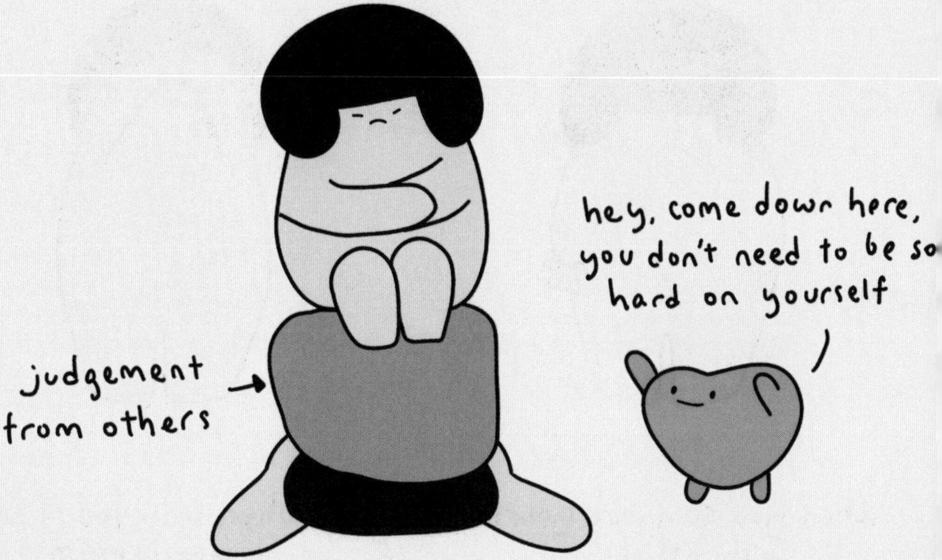
judgement from others
hey, come down here, you don't need to be so hard on yourself

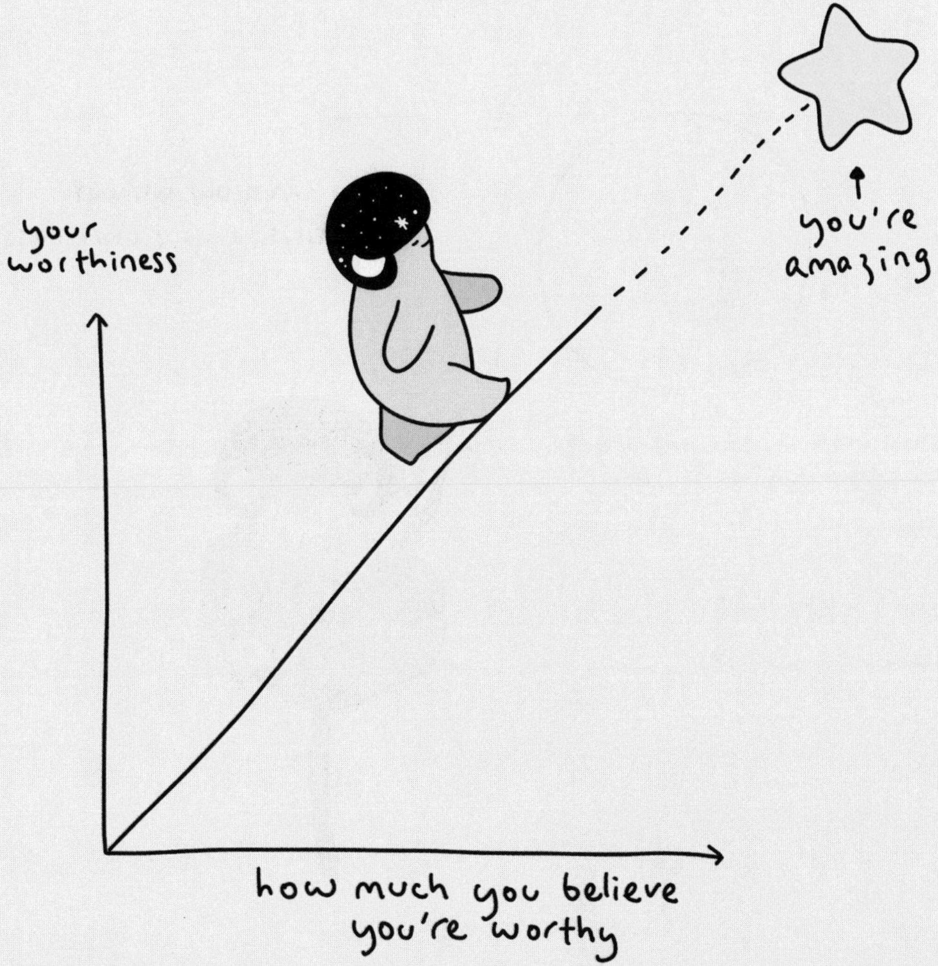
your worthiness
you're amazing
how much you believe you're worthy

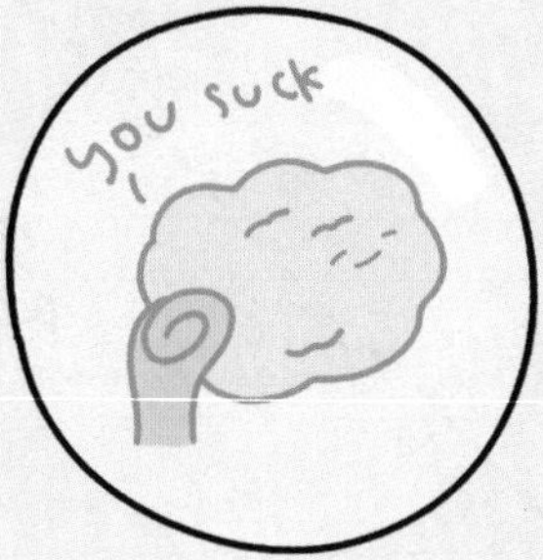
you suck

you can grow without
criticising your worthiness

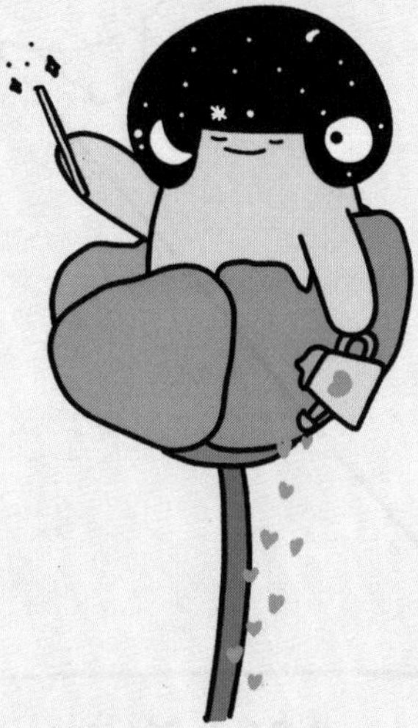

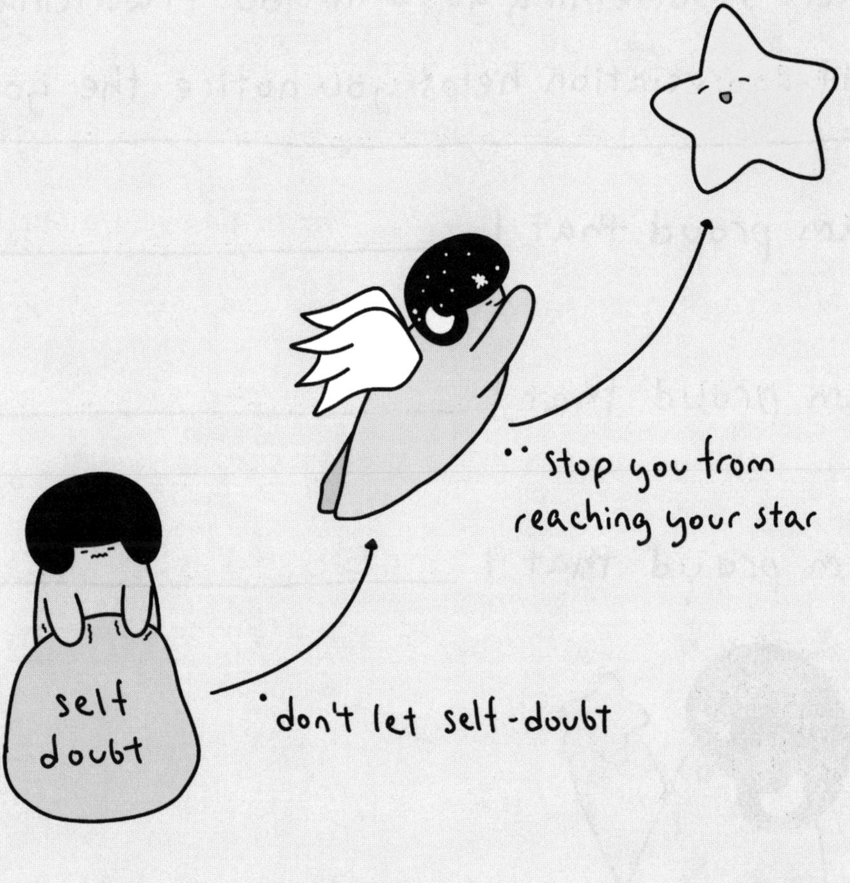
self doubt
don't let self-doubt
.. stop you from reaching your star

There's something good in you. Practicing self-appreciation helps you notice the good

I am proud that I _____

I am proud that I _____

I am proud that I _____

CHAPTER FOUR

GOOD DAYS ARE ON THEIR WAY

taking care of yourself during hard times,

and looking forward to the future—

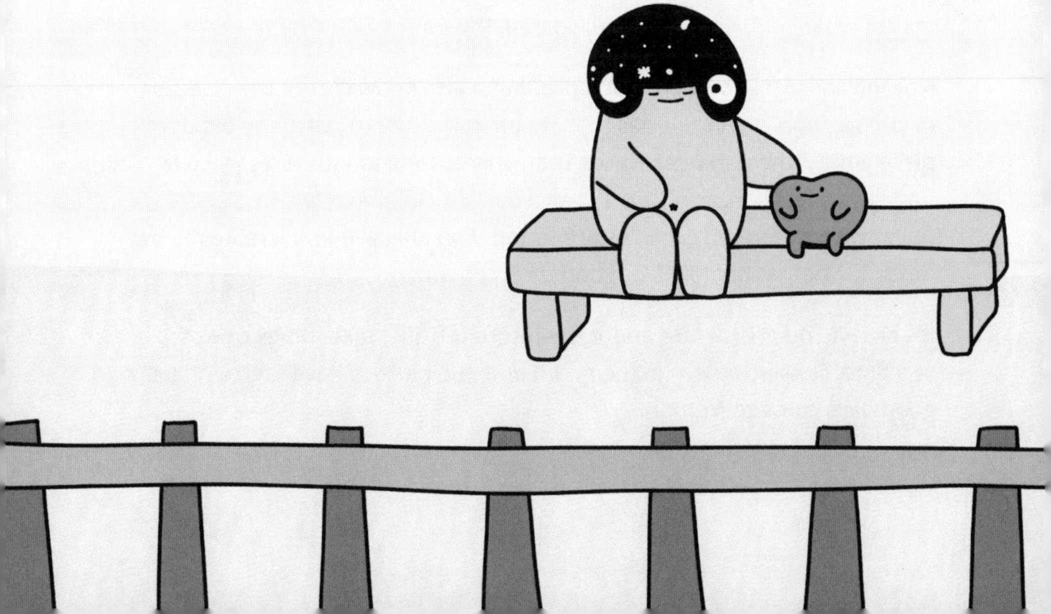

Taking Care of Yourself During Hard Times, and Looking Toward to the Future

When I was young, I imagined myself to be a prophet who could make all preparations before bad things happened. I didn't like change very much, and the uncertainty of life scared me. To be exact, the potential of having bad days haunted me. I had experienced them before, so I knew what I would feel if they came. I felt it would be super nice if I just knew everything that was going to happen ahead of time, and then... Wait! Assuming I could predict everything, didn't this mean the results would be fixed? That no matter what I did, how much I prepared, the future would be the same?

Now obviously I know I am not a prophet. I also know it's not the forecast or preparation for hard times that I need, but a way to get me to a better place amidst the darkness where I can stay as long as I want. Yes, I have bad days, I feel bad, and I am still afraid of the unknown future. But the unknown is where possibilities are found. And I believe I can create my own destiny, whether bad days or good days come.

It's okay if you are unsure about the future too, just take things one step at a time. Flowers bloom in their own time. Be patient, have faith, and let good days come to fruition.

it might look scary, not knowing what's inside
but within awaits infinite possibilities ☆

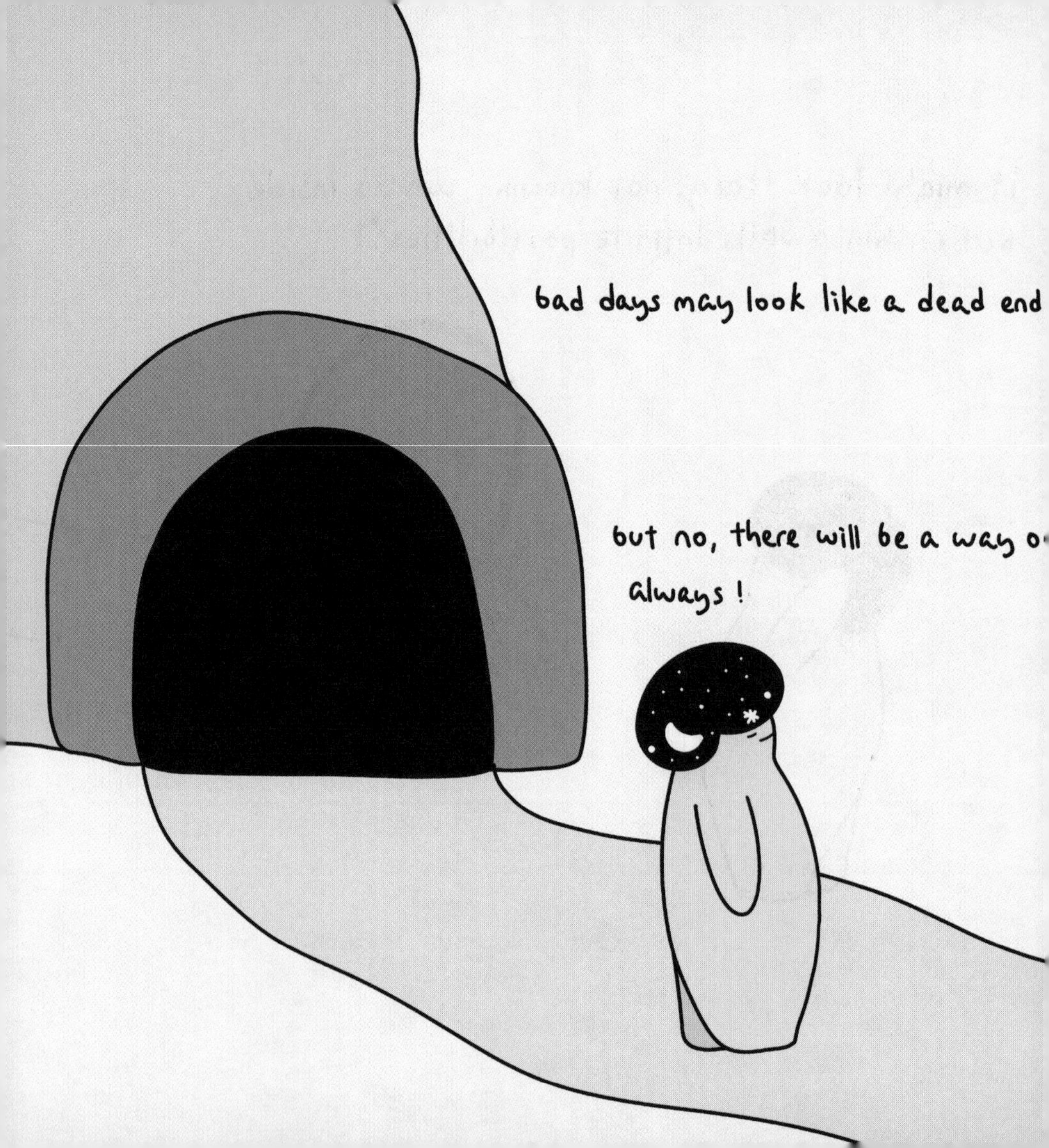
bad days may look like a dead end
but no, there will be a way o
always !

yes. there's a big challenge.
and yes, there will be a big star
for you

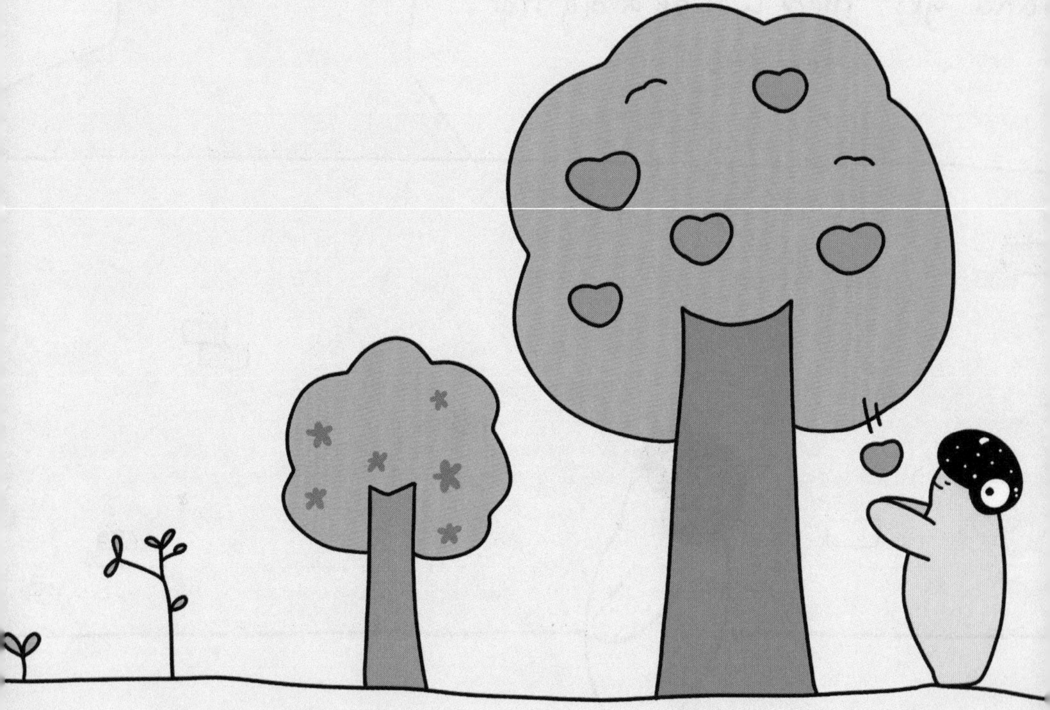

don't rush, give it time, your good days will come

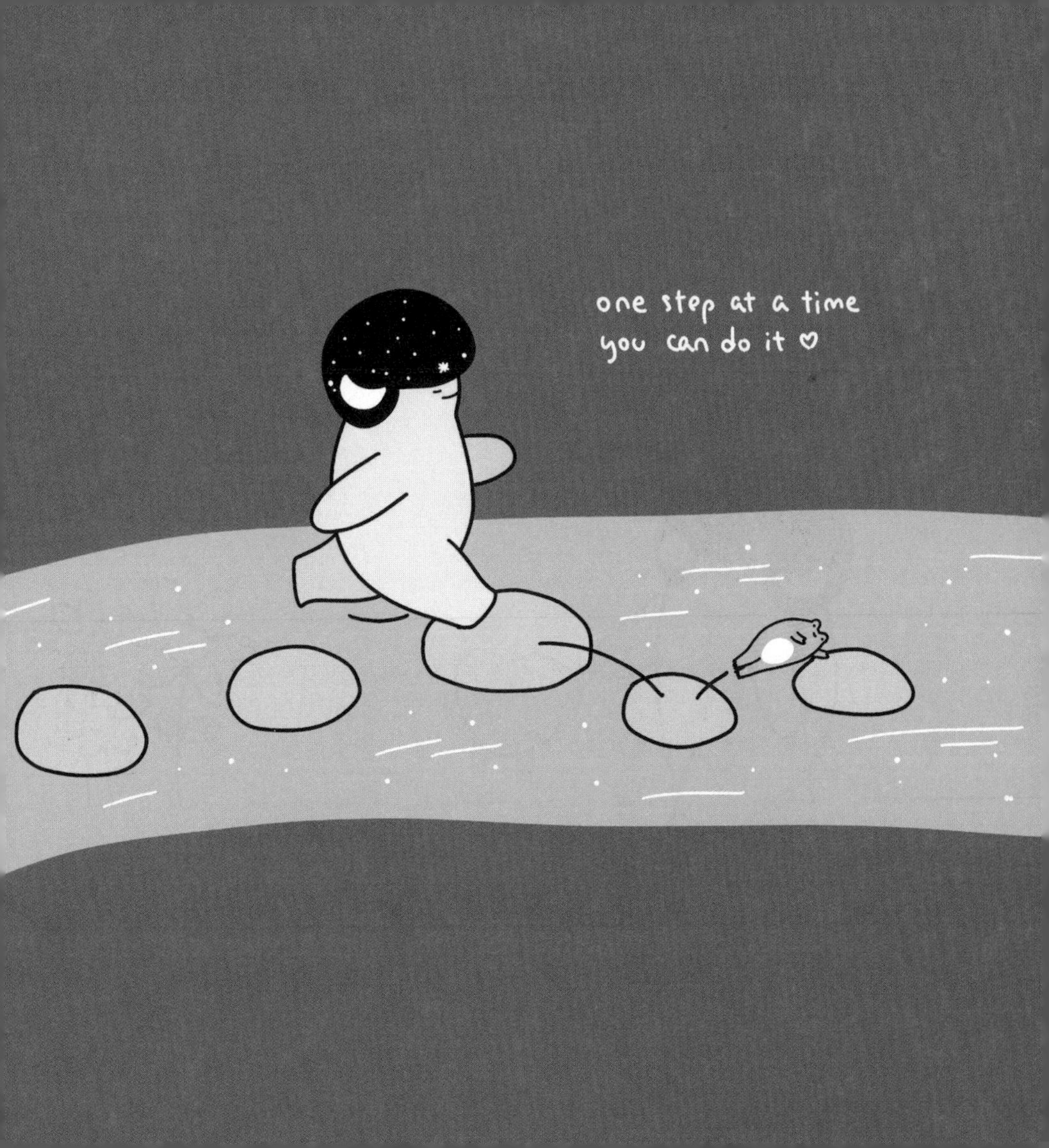
one step at a time
you can do it ♡

KEEP GOING
≷this is how you reach good days≷

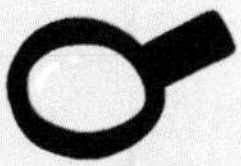

if you can't find happiness
out there

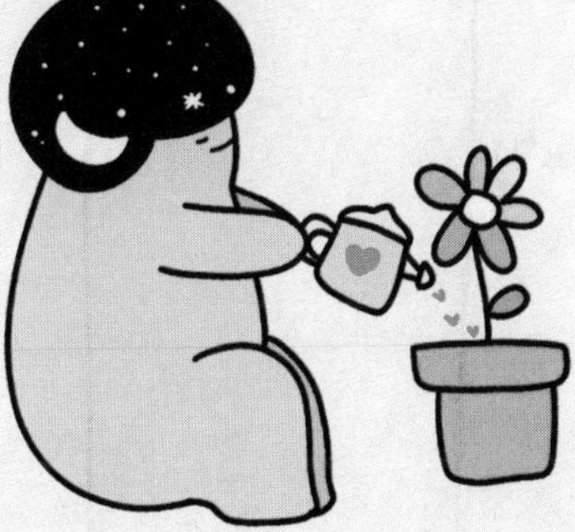

grow it yourself

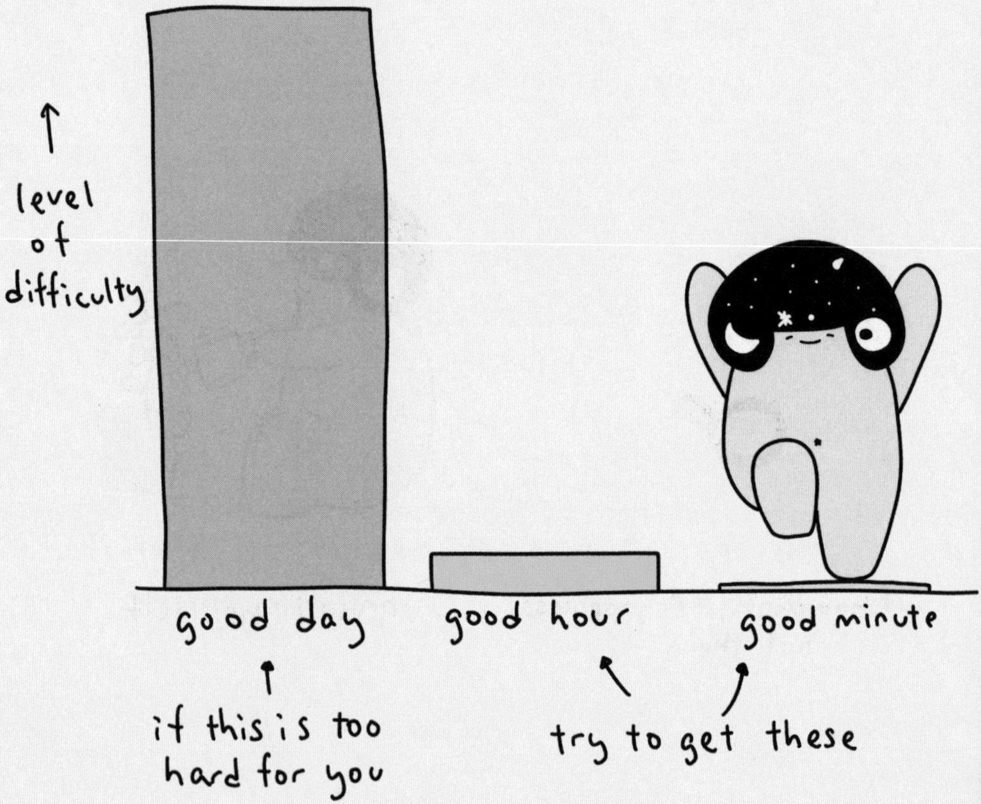
level of difficulty
good day
good hour
good minute
if this is too hard for you
try to get these

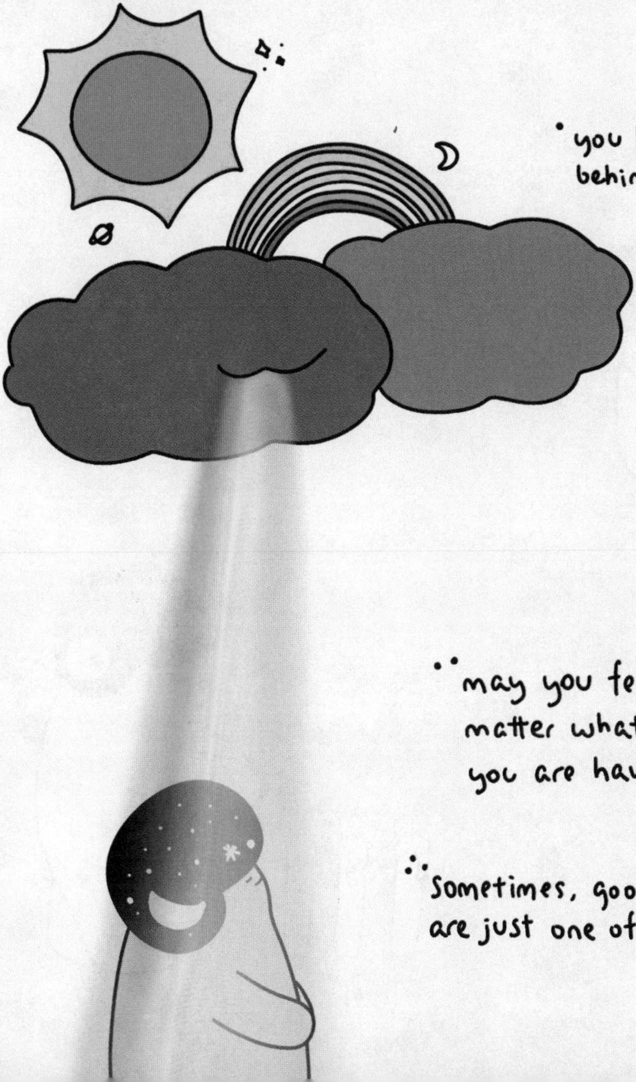

• you know there's magic behind the clouds

•• may you feel the magic no matter what kind of days you are having

∴ Sometimes, good days or bad days are just one of the perspectives

if your current thoughts about
a bad day aren't easing your day

try to accept that today is
a bad day, and do something
about it

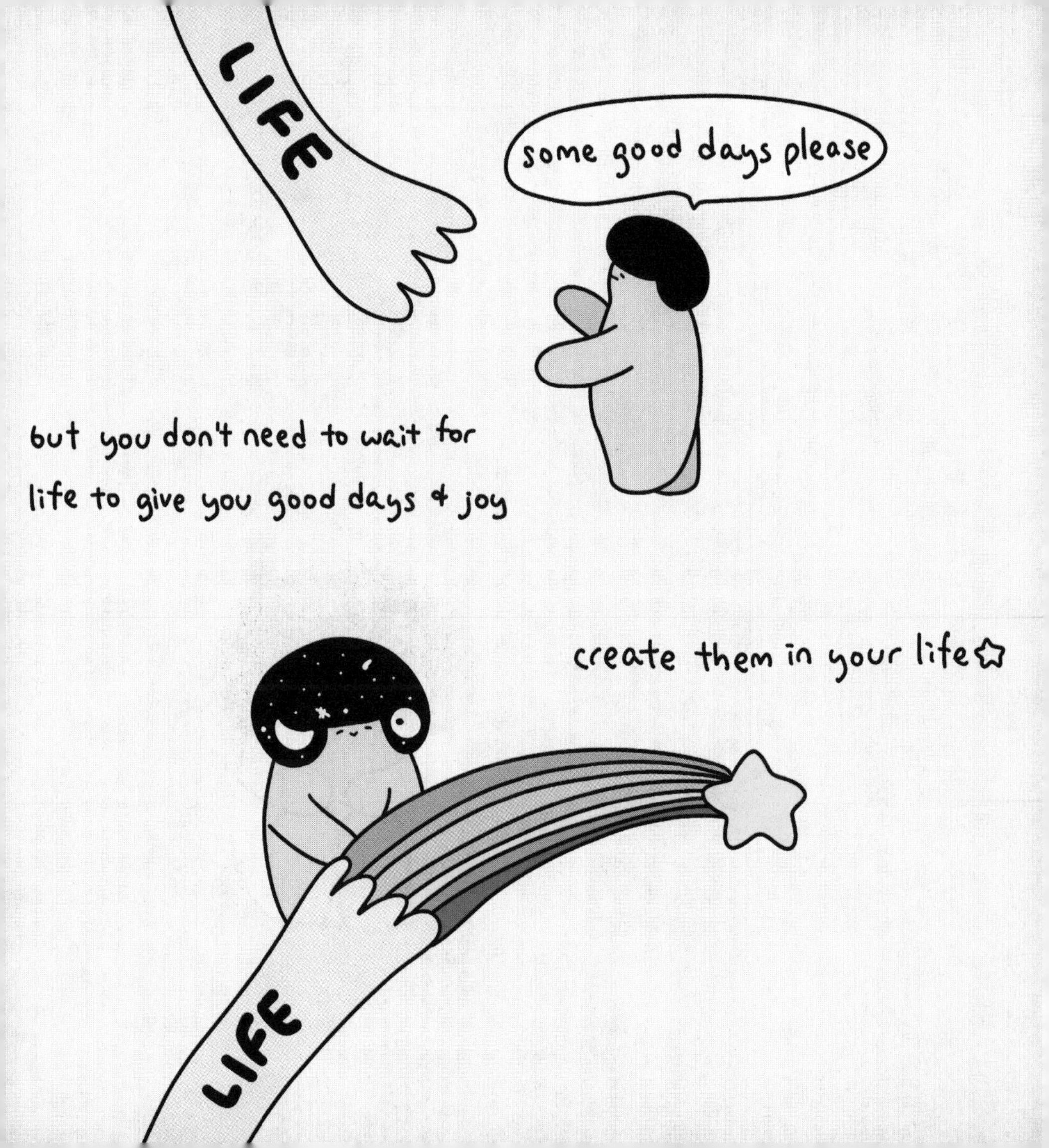
LIFE
some good days please
but you don't need to wait for life to give you good days & joy
create them in your life ☆
LIFE

maybe that little light isn't bringing you out from a bad day completely, BUT it isn't useless, it is here to remind you there's always hope

One common question we ask during difficult times is "When will better days come?" We are looking for the due date, reassuring ourselves that we will finally be free and happy again when they arrive. We expect good days to come in a heartbeat, but are disappointed over and over again. We complain about our challenges, wishing for better, but it doesn't help at all. While doing this clearly states what we want, unfortunately it doesn't just happen the *way* we want. Isn't it called the law of attraction? Aren't you supposed to think about the good days, and boom, good days come? Sometimes not...

This was a difficult lesson for me, until I heard about "The Backwards Law." A modern philosopher, Alan Watts, suggested the idea that the more we pursue feeling better all the time, the less satisfied we become, as pursuing something only reinforces the fact that we lack it in the first place.

It's no wonder we don't feel better when we wish for brighter times, as it reminds us how hard our current situation is. The more we focus on the struggle, the more difficult it is live with.

But can we still do something about this?

The question is the key to the answer. If this question isn't bringing us to the place we want to go, let's change the question.

questions are the keys of answers

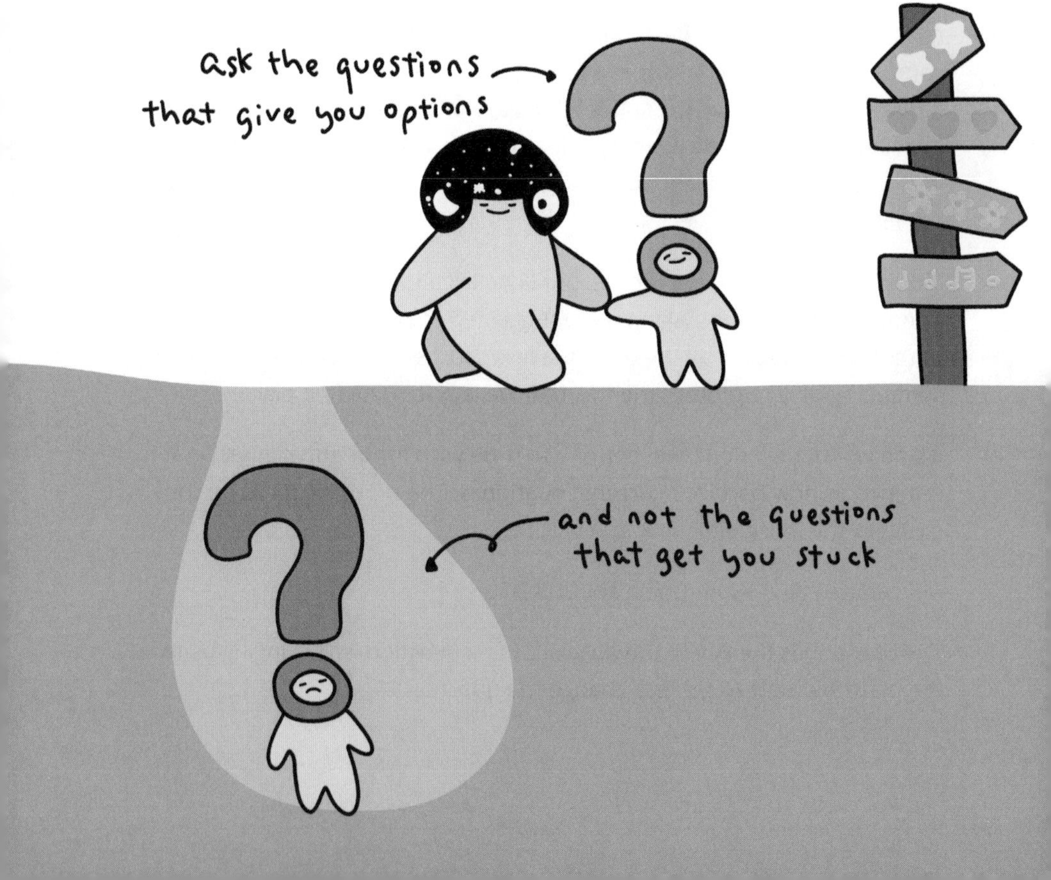
ask the questions that give you options
and not the questions that get you stuck

What can I do to make today better?

How can I reach the good days?

What did I do last time to get through bad days?

Do I need to get help?

There are many questions that can inspire us, and guide us to a more positive way of thinking. We don't have to live in the place of lack to achieve something great. Whenever you are wishing for good days, remember to center yourself. By calming your body, and feeling your heart, magic happens.

every time you breathe in,
imagine the light of good days coming to you

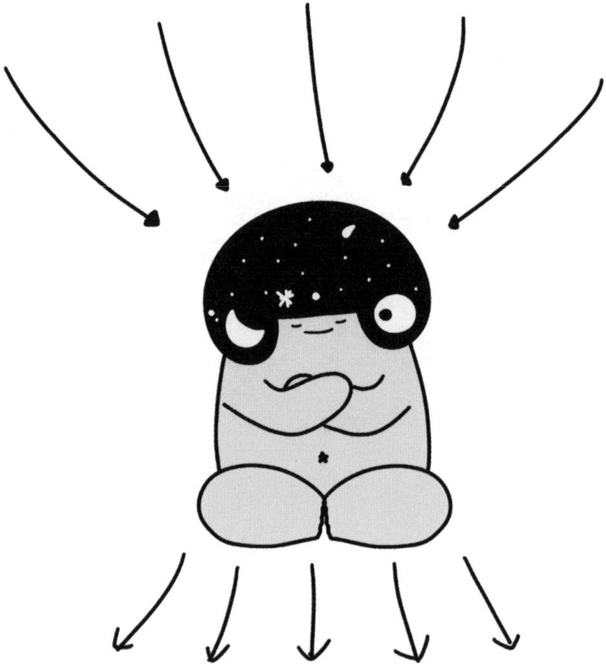

every time you breathe out,
release the heaviness of bad days

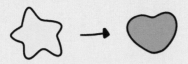

if I think good things are coming,
I'll be happy

positive thoughts and happiness come in pairs

so hold tight to the good things in your
heart, the star is coming

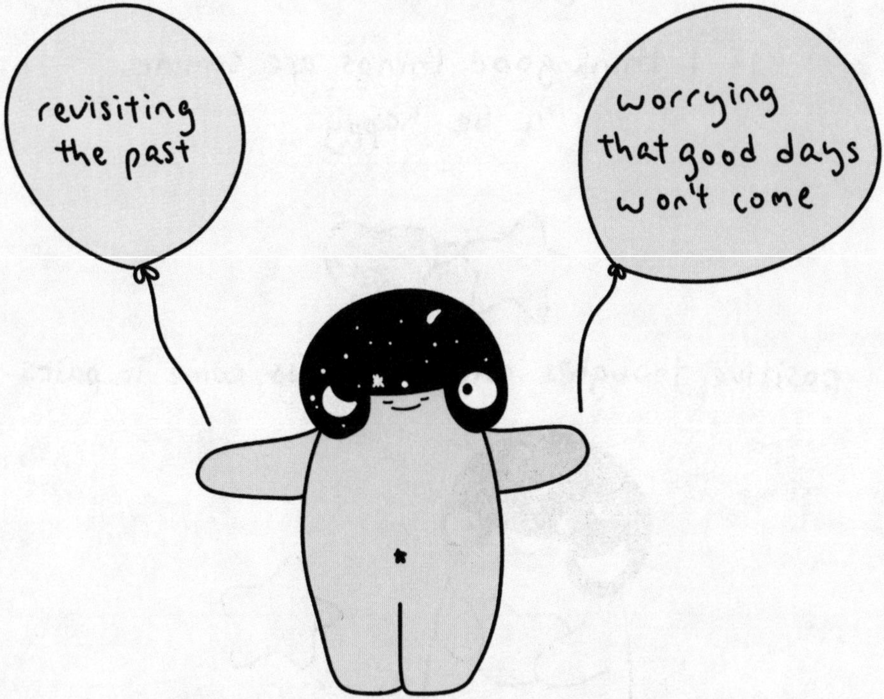
revisiting the past
worrying that good days won't come

live in the moment
and you'll find you don't need to define your days

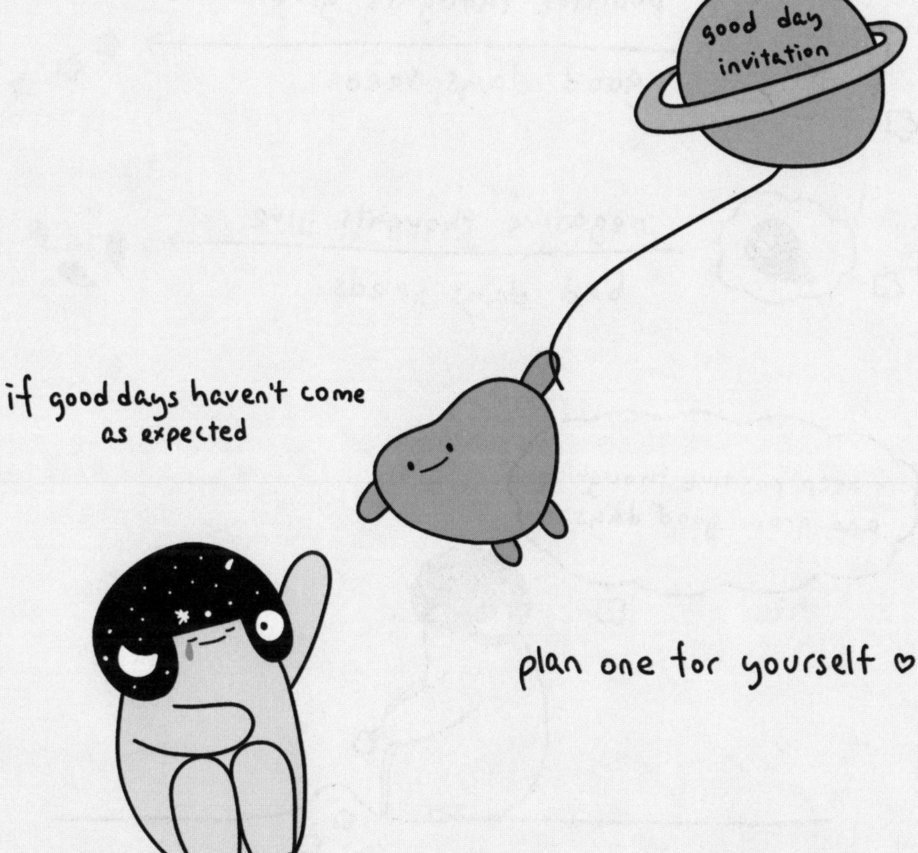
good day invitation
if good days haven't come as expected
plan one for yourself ♡

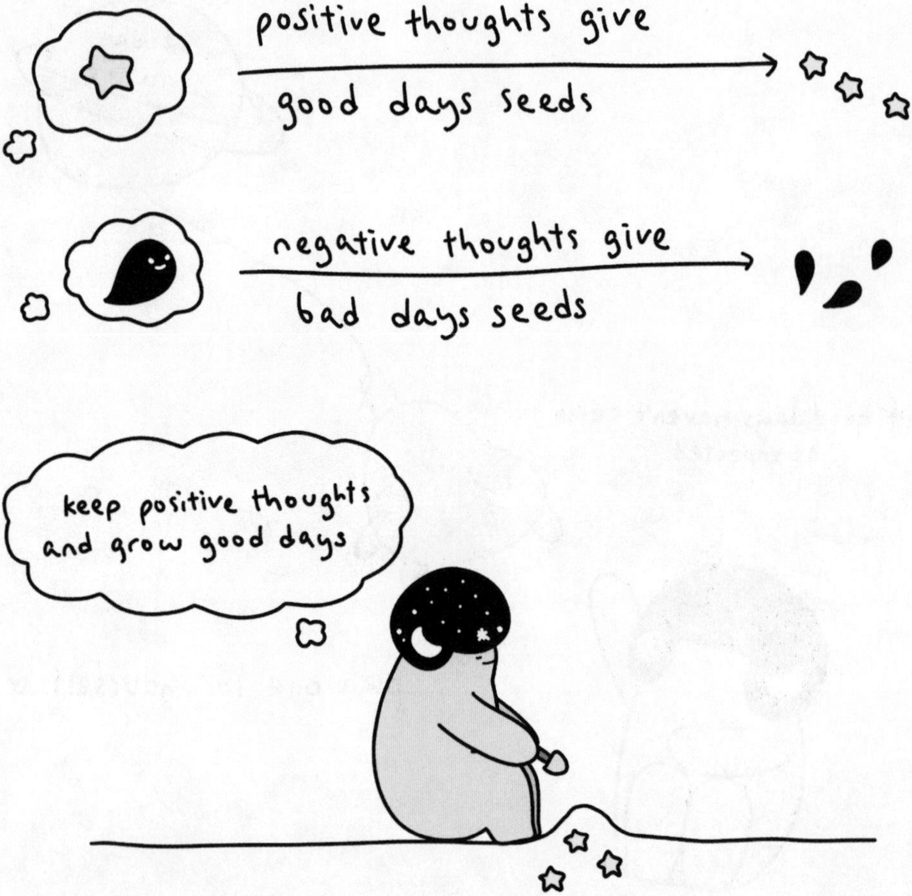
positive thoughts give
good days seeds
negative thoughts give
bad days seeds
keep positive thoughts and grow good days

sometimes carrying the past is
preventing you from having a good day

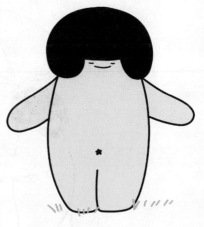

be present, maybe you're
having a good day already

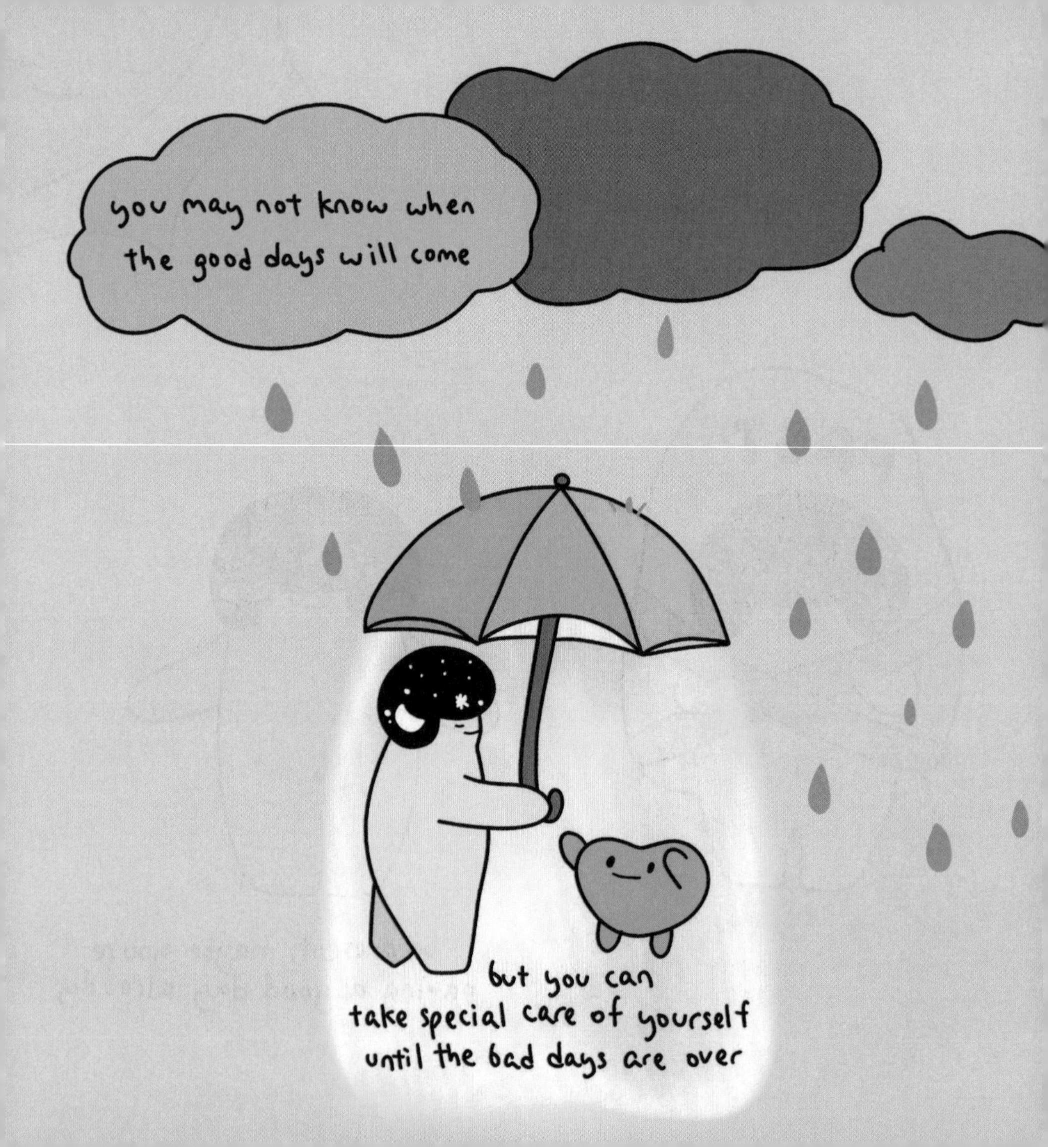
you may not know when
the good days will come
but you can
take special care of yourself
until the bad days are over

remember your heart is always here
for you, and this is where good days start

good days will come
be ready for them

a positive attitude helps
good days find you☆

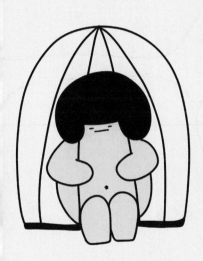

it's difficult to find joy
in what you don't love

it's okay to search for
what can make you happy

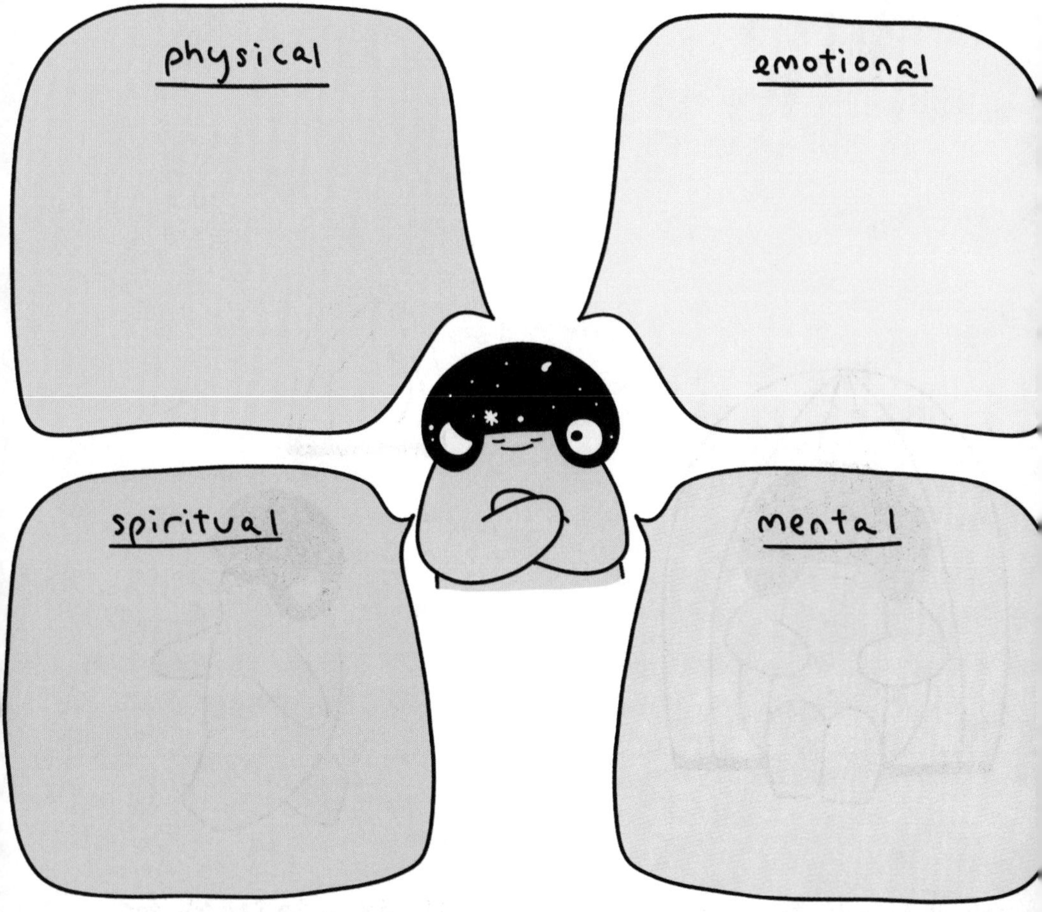
physical
emotional
spiritual
mental

set intentions, instead of goals,
they can make your days easier

what will you say to your friends
when they have a bad day?

now, use these tender
words to warm your heart

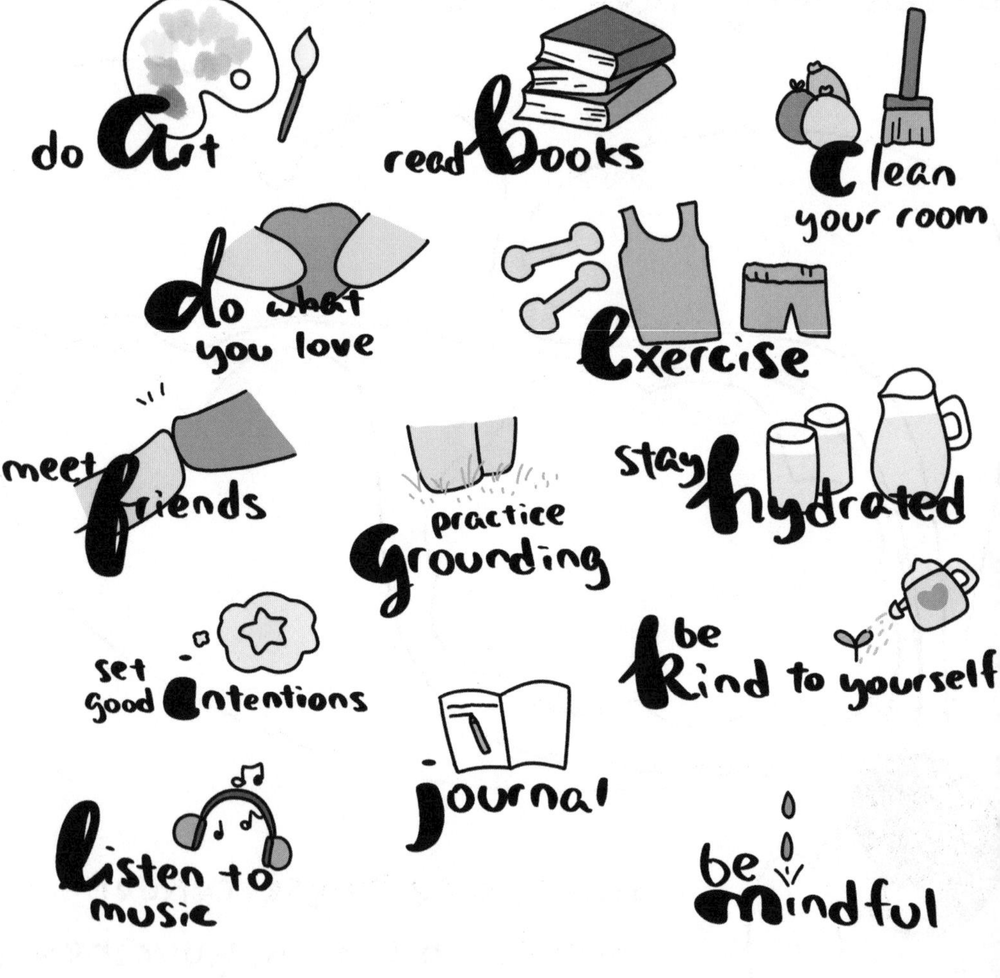

do Art
read books
Clean your room
do what you love
Exercise
meet friends
practice Grounding
stay hydrated
set good intentions
be Kind to yourself
journal
listen to music
be mindful

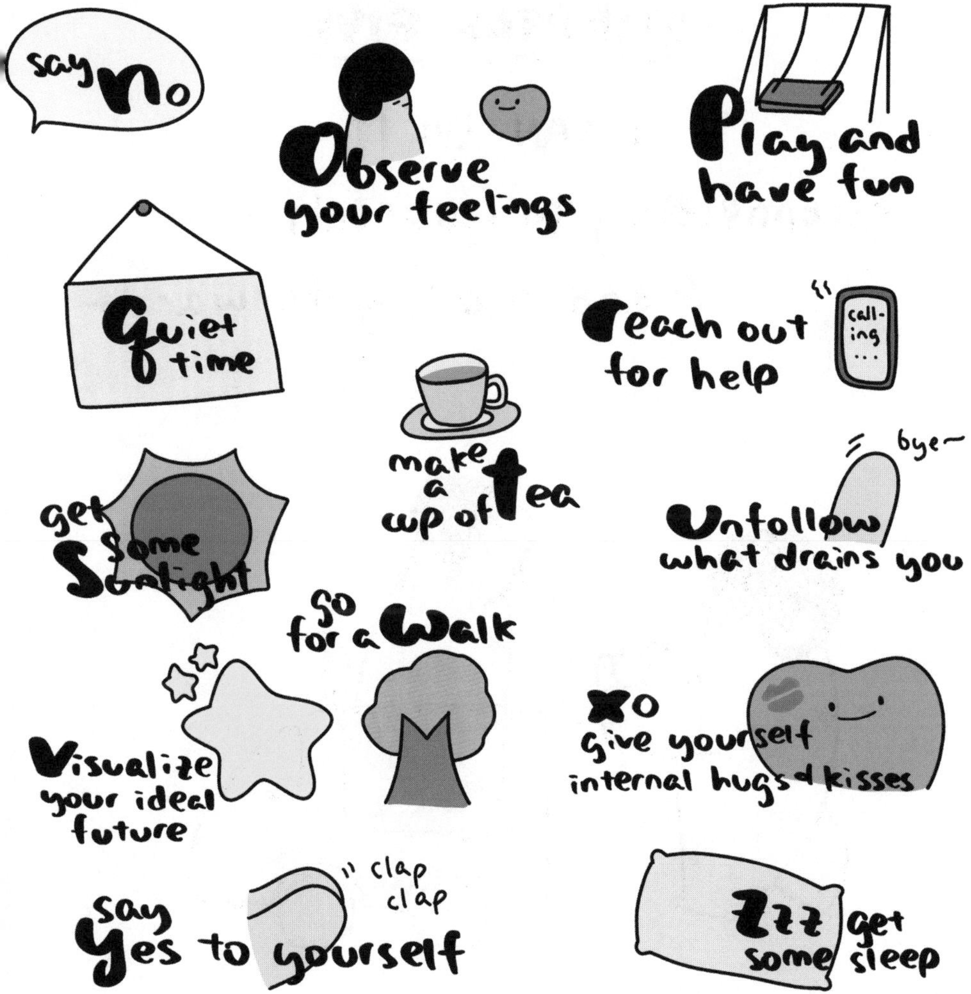
say no
Observe your feelings
Play and have fun
Quiet time
Reach out for help
call-ing...
make a cup of tea
bye~
Unfollow what drains you
get some Sunlight
go for a Walk
XO give yourself internal hugs & kisses
Visualize your ideal future
clap clap
say Yes to yourself
ZZZ get some sleep

CHAPTER FIVE

I CAN DO IT
-reconnecting to yourself
and moving forward-

Reconnecting to Yourself and Moving Forward

Many of us feel guilty when we put ourselves first, especially when we know there are many others suffering in the world, including our Mother Earth. We see many kind people dedicate their time to serving their community, and shining their stars to make a better world. Should we just stop thinking about ourselves and start doing something?

Some of us don't believe we deserve love or just simply self-hate so much that we don't even want to spend time focusing on ourselves. Self-care seems to be a really difficult task. Who *would* be passionate about doing nice things for someone they didn't like?

Some people try very hard to love themselves, but they think they have made no progress, and wonder if they should give up.

I know you must have heard so much about self-care, why you need it, what activities you can do, and how self-care can benefit your life. So for a moment, let's talk about having a *lack* of self-care, and observe what this could do to us.

Physical Self-Care

Self-care is health care. If you stop caring for your body, it will complain in ways you don't want. Poor health means a lack of energy. The kind of energy you need to do what you love, to feel the good in the world, to protect yourself from the bad vibes—and the kind of energy you need to take care of your loved ones.

Emotional Self-Care

Emotions help us discover more about ourselves, what we love, what we fear, what to avoid, what to do more of. What will happen if we ignore the signs they give us? We may become numb to both happiness and sadness, we may cling to the negative emotions and let them consume us; eventually, we may take the negative emotions out on the people we love and hurt our relationships.

Mental Self-Care

There are so many people struggling with their mental health, working very hard to survive difficult times, and seeking better days. So what happens when you don't care for your mental health? Bad days are probably dominant, and we may only experience good days by luck.

Spiritual Self-Care

This doesn't necessarily need to be religious. You can consider spiritual self-care as something related to your soul, the connection you have with God or the universe, your life's purpose, your faith, your consciousness... If you quit this part, there will be a big gap between yourself and a meaningful life.

What if we *do* practice self-care? Does that mean we won't experience any of the above? Things might fluctuate, but we will experience balance and contentment more often when we do practice self-care. Only by knowing where we are and where we want to go are we able to choose our way forward.

Some people declare their failure too soon—truthfully, I believe it's always too soon to declare failure. As long as there's life, there's hope. Be willing to see your progress, even if your progress is tiny, it will help you to move forward. Self-encouragement always helps!

The truth is, self-care isn't selfish. On the contrary, self-care is an aspect of selflessness. Consider the impact you can have on the world when you practice self-care.

When you treat your physical body well, you can literally bring happiness to the world. You will shine when you do what you love, and this gives light to other people. You will also have more energy to help people in need.

When you have a good relationship with your emotions, you will understand yourself and others better. This brings more kindness and compassion to the world.

When you take good care of your mental health, you will have easier days. Your experience can help others cope with their own mental health issues, too.

When you connect with your soul, you know being who you are isn't selfish, but aligns you with your higher self, and allows your stars to shine. You understand how to live your life fully, and set a good example to the people around you.

True self-care isn't about doing whatever you want and neglecting all others. True self-care is taking good care of yourself so that the best of you can shine outward to the world.

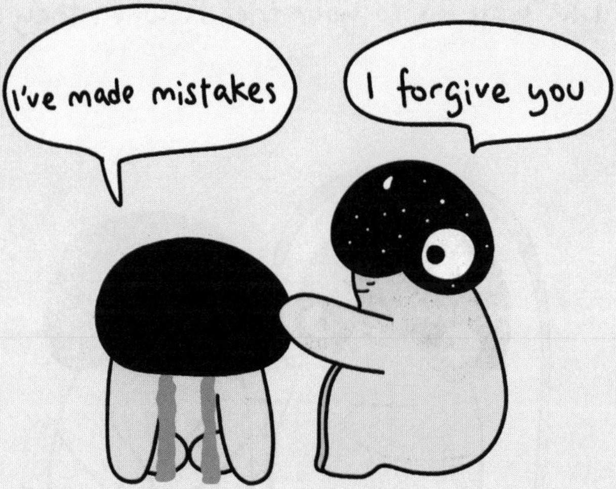
I've made mistakes
I forgive you

forgiving yourself is one of the biggest gifts you can give to yourself

give yourself a big, warm smile and support,
just like you do to your friends when they need it

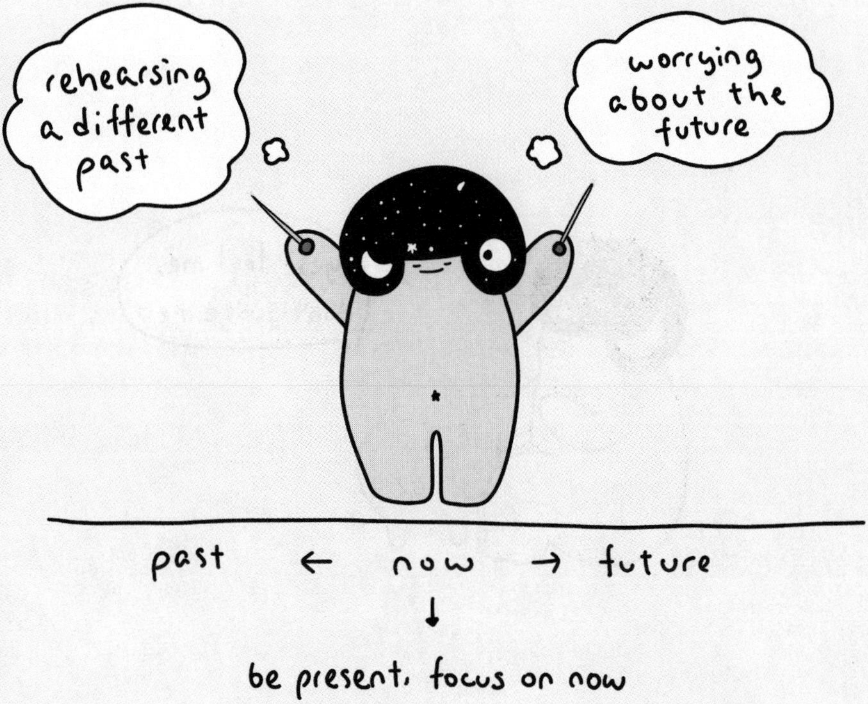
rehearsing a different past
worrying about the future
past ← now → future
↓
be present. focus on now

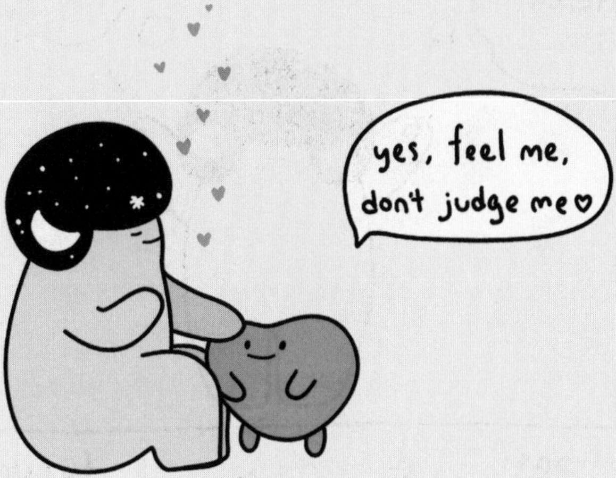
yes, feel me,
don't judge me♡

every time you don't know what to do

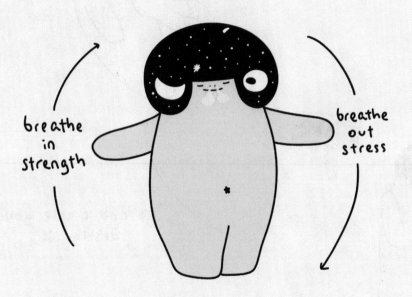

breathe
in
strength

breathe
out
stress

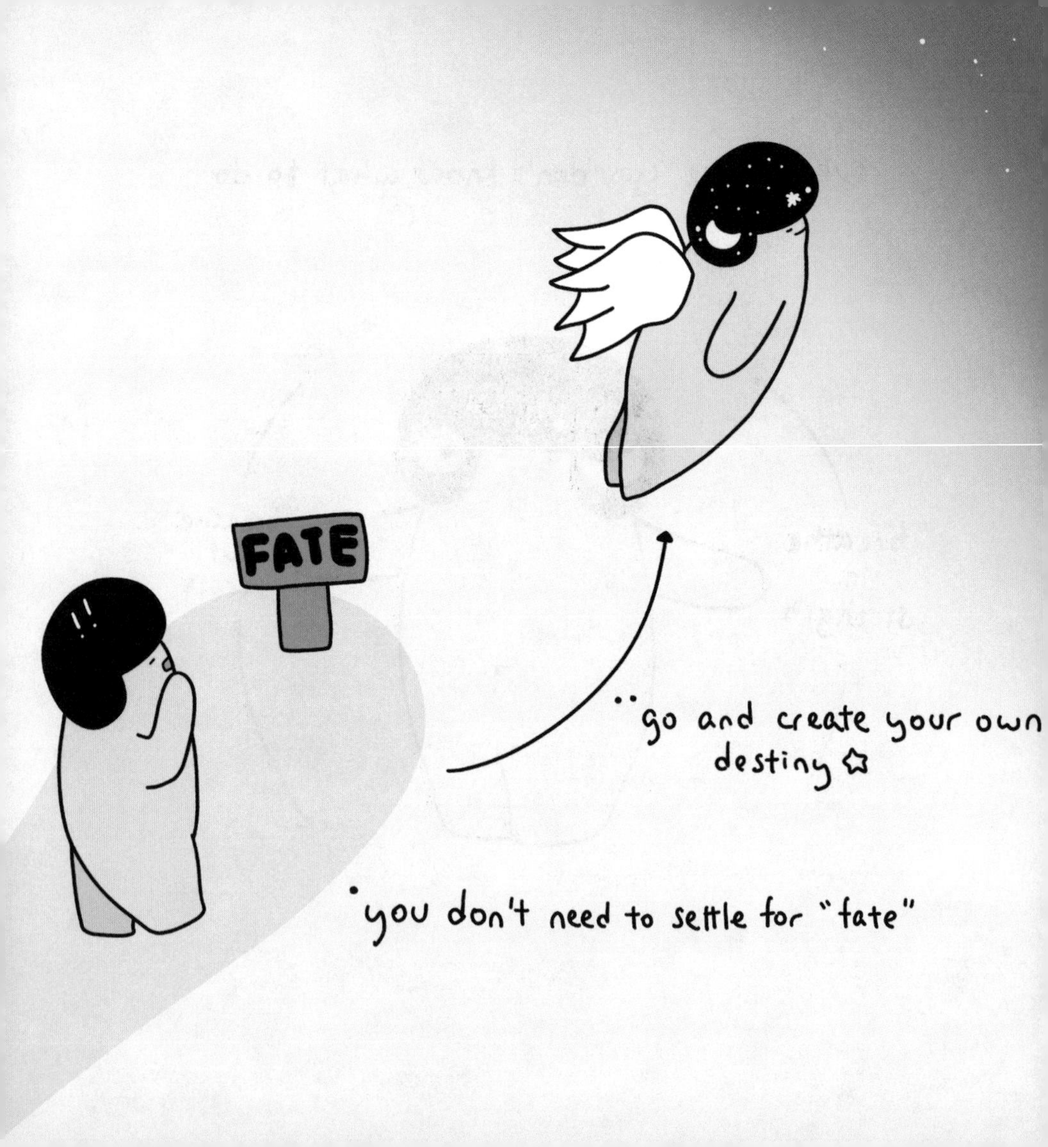
FATE
..go and create your own destiny ✩
•you don't need to settle for "fate"

it's okay to move on . and go adventure

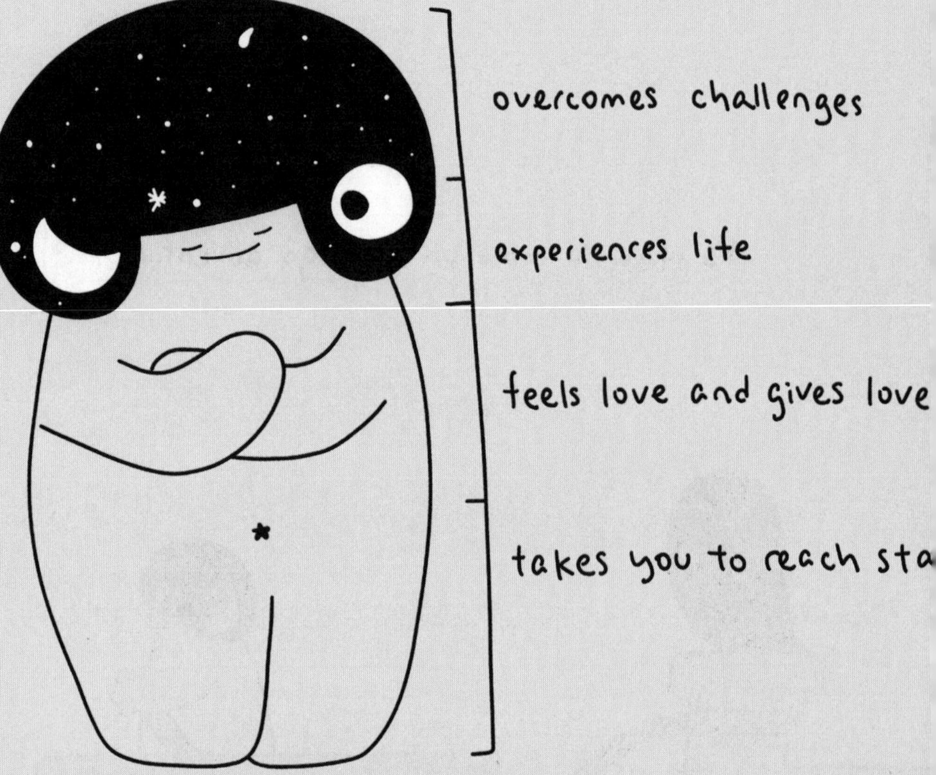
overcomes challenges
experiences life
feels love and gives love
takes you to reach sta

take good care of your body,
because it's with you no matter what

let love heal, it always can

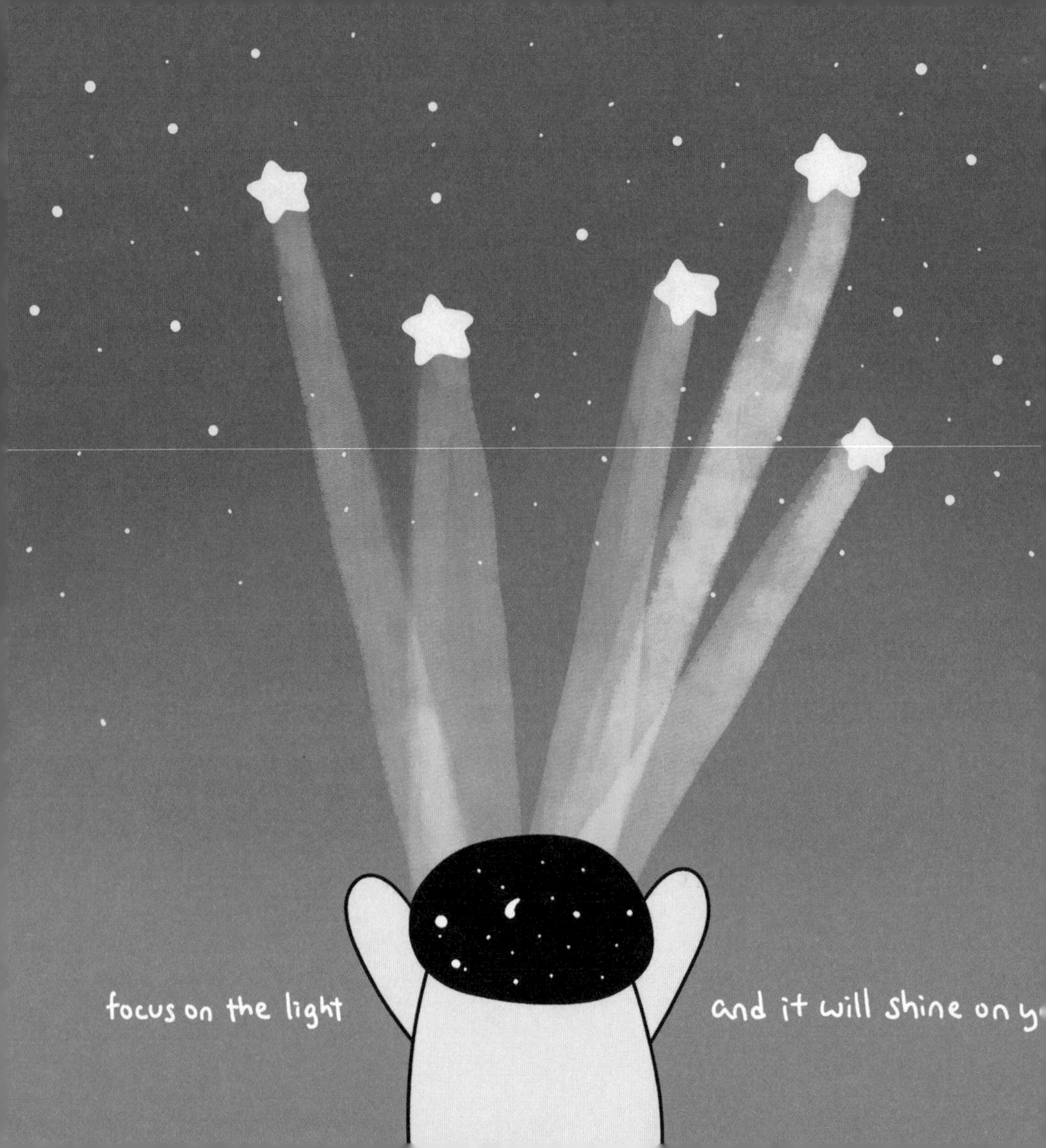
focus on the light
and it will shine on y

be aware of what you let in
choose wisely

you are always ready to fly
drop what doesn't serve you

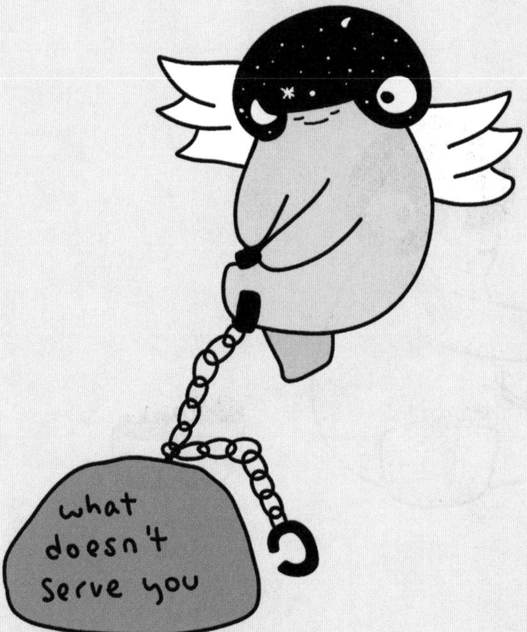
what doesn't serve you

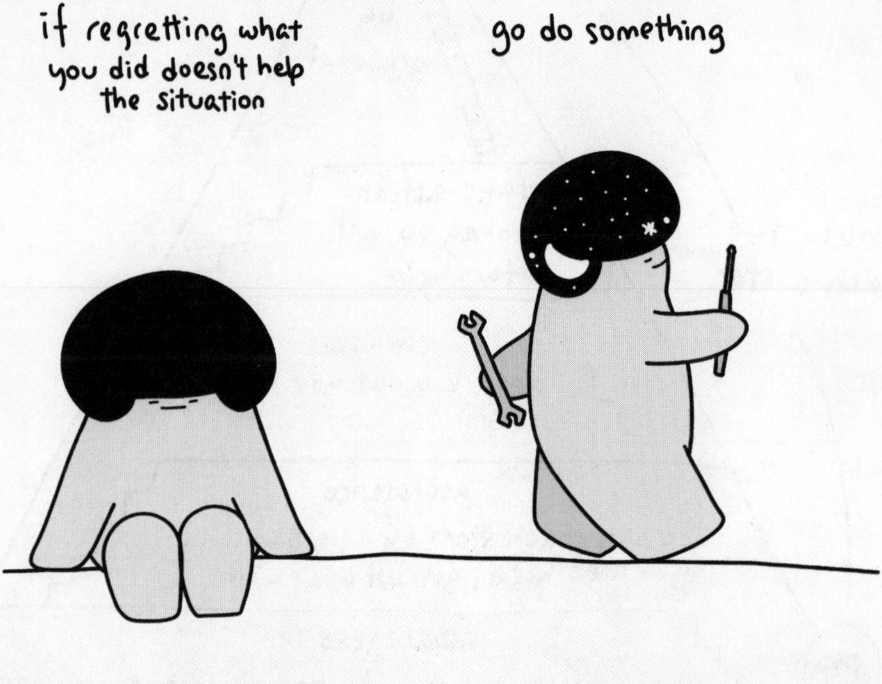
if regretting what you did doesn't help the situation
go do something

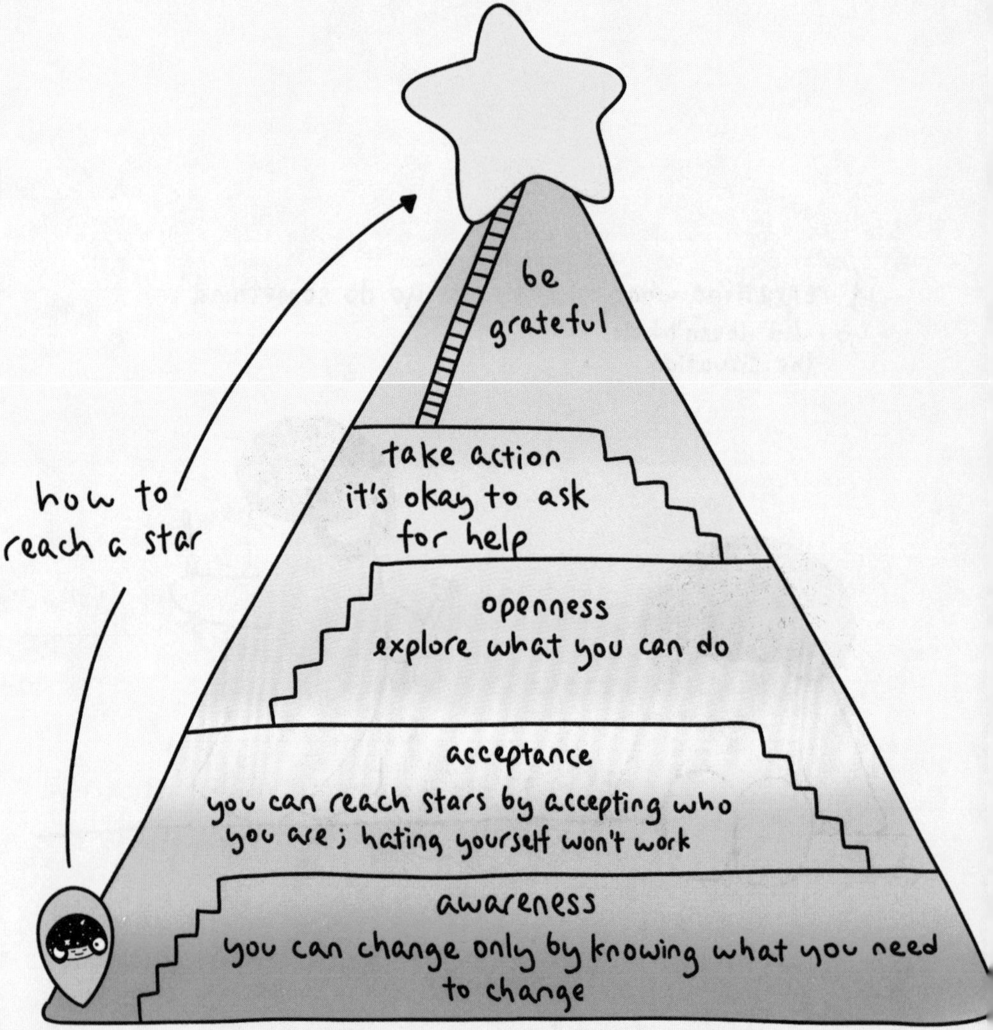
how to
reach a star
be
grateful
take action
it's okay to ask
for help
openness
explore what you can do
acceptance
you can reach stars by accepting who
you are ; hating yourself won't work
awareness
you can change only by knowing what you need
to change

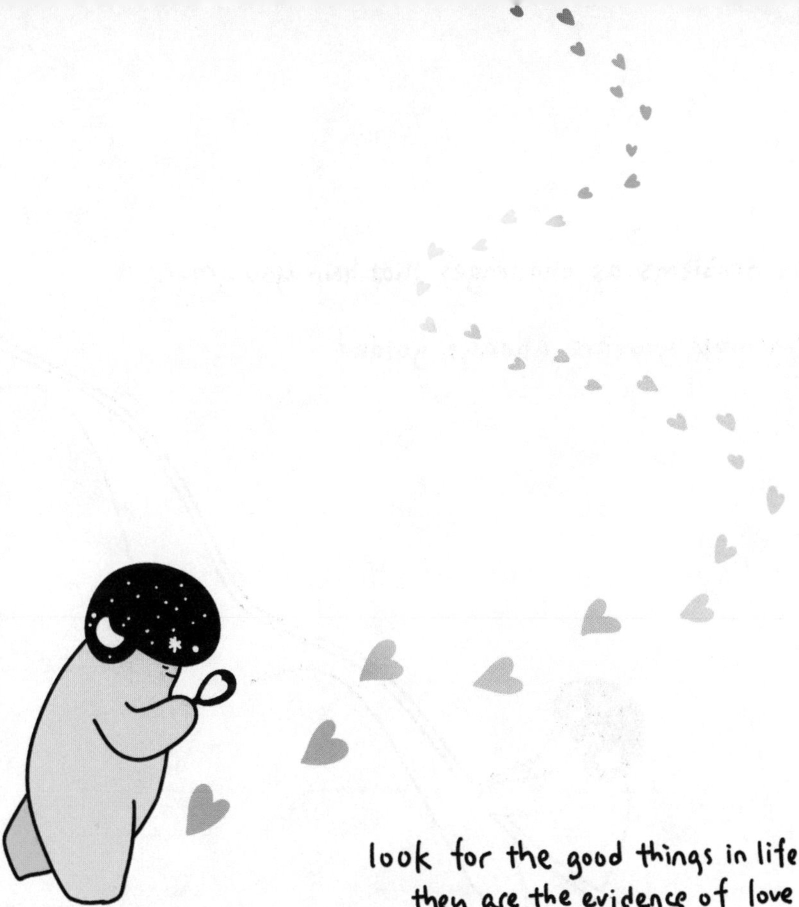

look for the good things in life,
they are the evidence of love

see problems as challenges that help you grow,

remember you are always guided

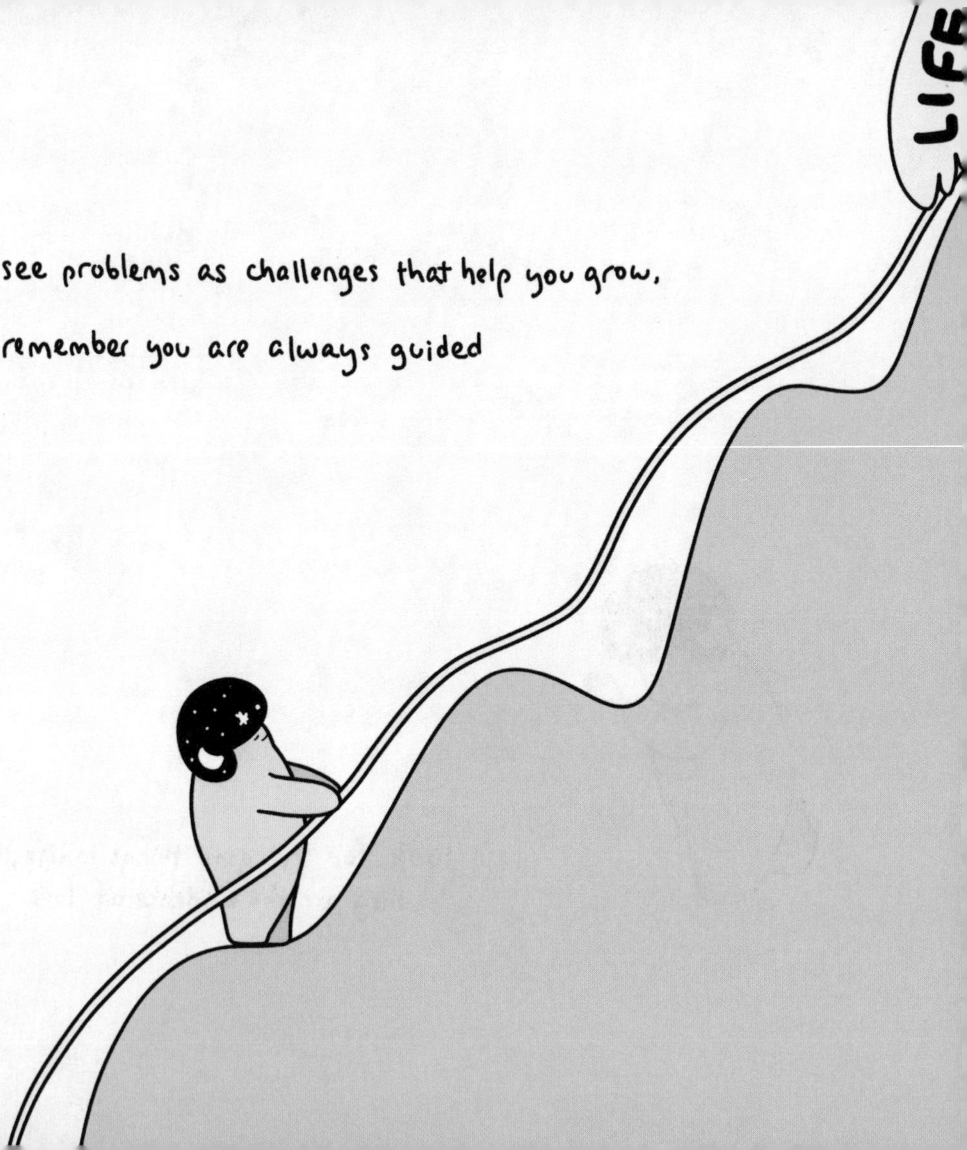
LIFE

even if it seems nice, if you don't feel good holding on to it, it's okay to let go

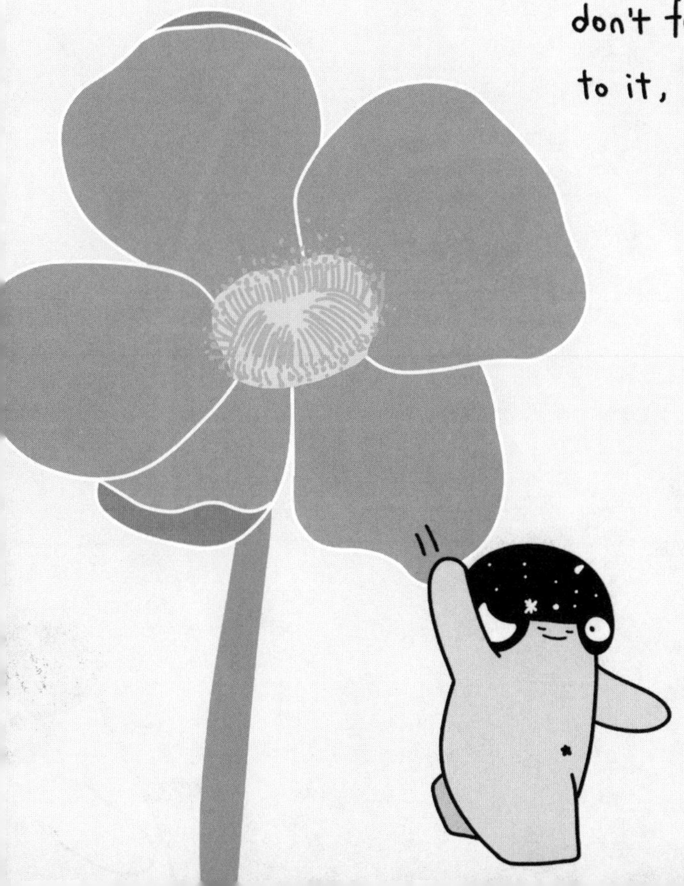

HOW A POSITIVE BELIEF IS BORN

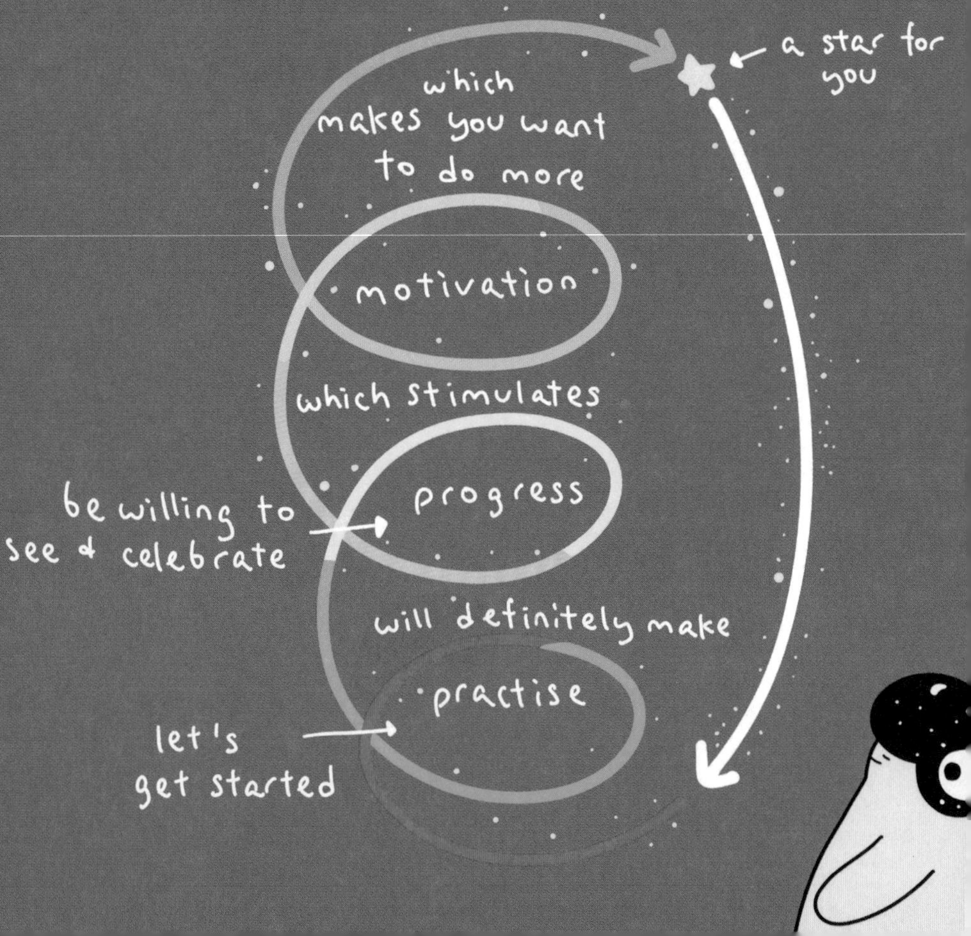

a star for you
which makes you want to do more
motivation
which stimulates
progress
be willing to see & celebrate
will definitely make
practise
let's get started

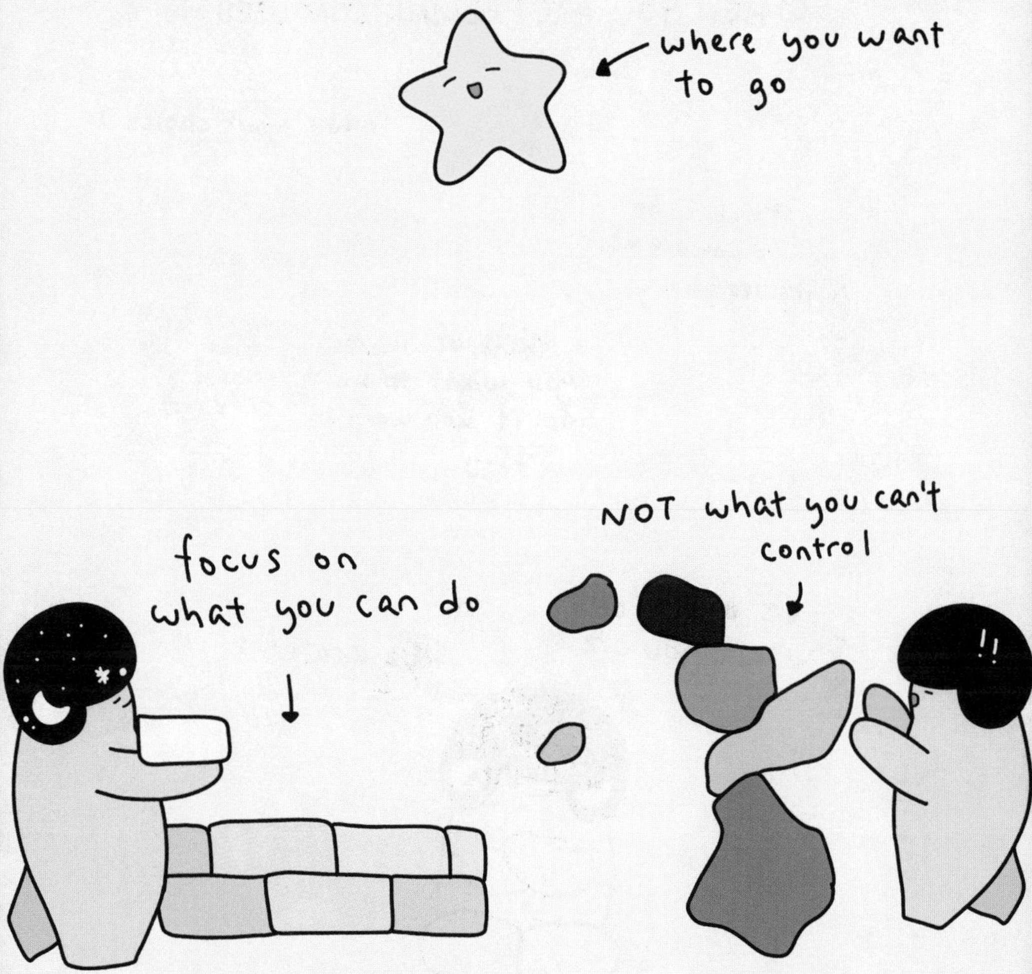
where you want to go
focus on what you can do
NOT what you can't control

WHEN YOU ARE FEELING CONFUSED

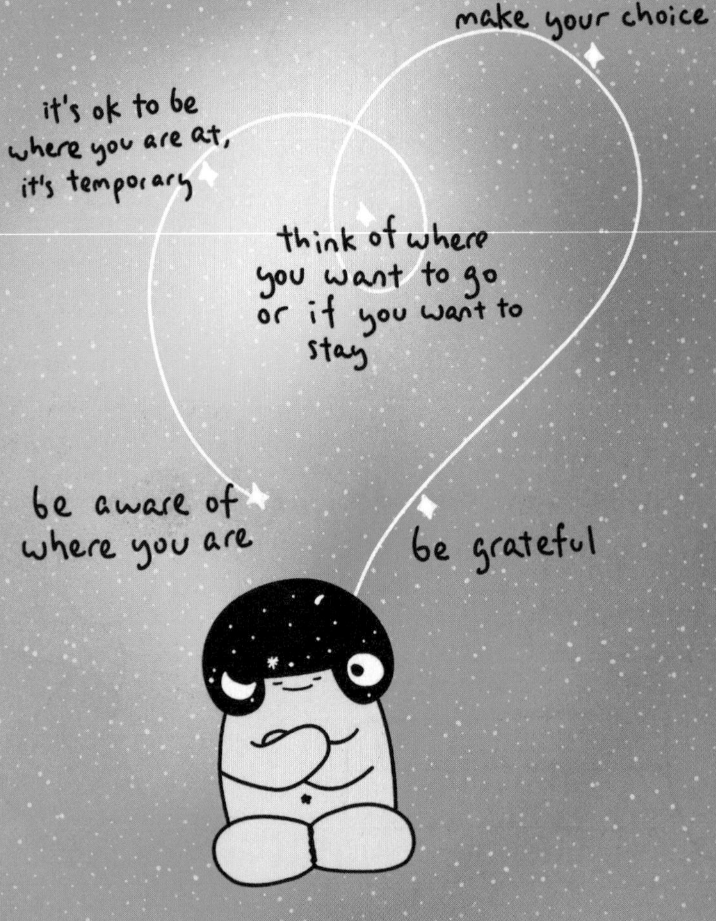
make your choice
it's ok to be where you are at, it's temporary
think of where you want to go or if you want to stay
be aware of where you are
be grateful

write a love note or a motivation note
to yourself every day

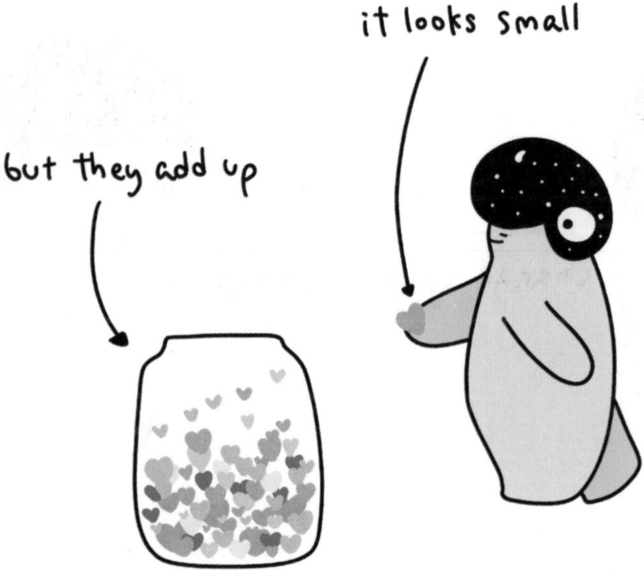
it looks small
but they add up

change your posture

change your feelings

stand up straight and stretch a bit ˘‿˘

use your 5 senses help reach your heart

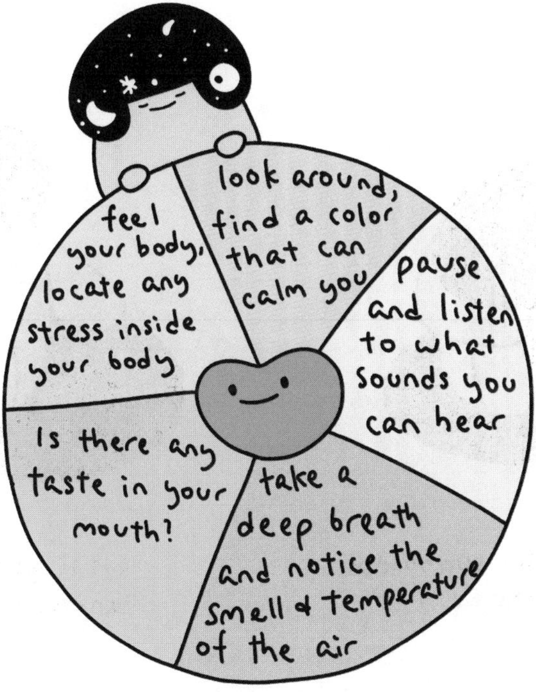

look around, find a color that can calm you
pause and listen to what sounds you can hear
take a deep breath and notice the smell & temperature of the air
Is there any taste in your mouth?
feel your body, locate any stress inside your body

it feels bad to be surrounded
by negativity

but if you try to be
thankful for something

and keep planting
even more gratitude

negativity cannot harm
you anymore

Self-forgiveness can be hard, but it can be done. Start by noticing what you're struggling with, and send yourself some love

I forgive myself for _____

I forgive myself for _____

I forgive myself for _____

CHAPTER SIX

I PROMISE MYSELF...

-making self-love a habit-

Making Self-Love a Habit

Self-love was once like a myth to me. How could I practice loving myself when I actually didn't? Could someone really reach that level? What if I just couldn't do it? I wondered if there a way that didn't involve too much work. And if I got there one day, if I would finally live happily ever after.

With many doubts and questions, I started my self-love journey. But the reason I embarked on the journey at the time was not because I wanted to love myself more—I was just so done with my negative thoughts and emotions. I was living meaninglessly everyday, I had no motivation for anything, I couldn't find my purpose in my life, and even having fun was stressful for me. I hated this state of being, but the more I hated it, the more I was upset.

I didn't want to be like that at all.

One day, as my negative thoughts began automatically again, I wondered if there was a practical way to make them go away, instead of just praying for a magic pill to erase all of the unhappy things in my life. (By the way, erasing them never happened for me.) I guessed I just wanted to be happy again, and to not feel so low all of the time. Don't get me wrong—I understood that being generally happy doesn't guarantee a perfect life.

So I reached out for friends' support, read books, and took classes to learn about myself and try to change my negative thoughts. I wouldn't say this was an easy journey, but it was a magical one. Sometimes there were insightful perspectives, sometimes there were truths I didn't want to face. In spite of it all, I got closer to my heart, and began to understand why I need love and deserve love.

I came to realize self-love is not a destination, it's a journey. With a little bit more love for myself every day, I grew a little bit closer to my heart. There are still days I am far away from my heart, but most days I can reach it. Most importantly, however, for all of my days, I am around my heart, and it's around me. My heart is here for me, always.

Even now, I still can't guarantee to love myself 100 percent every day. But I do promise to give myself a little bit more love than yesterday. It's okay to give just 10 percent more, or even 1 percent more—it adds up. The gift behind the action is worth more than 100 percent.

There will be difficult periods in our lives, even we practice self-love. We can't control everything, but we don't have to resonate our inner world with the outside world. We don't need to drown ourselves in a sea of negativity, or even dip our toe in it, just because the waves are on our shore. Loving ourselves doesn't mean we will face no challenges. Loving ourselves means we have found a peaceful land to stand firmly on, even in a chaotic world. That piece of land is our heart.

Promise yourself that you will hold on tight to your heart in every situation in life, promise yourself you will keep focusing on the light even on dark days, and promise yourself that you will see and celebrate every little bit of progress.

before I make the decision

make sure you give yourself 3-4 options to choose from, so that you don't need to do something without choices

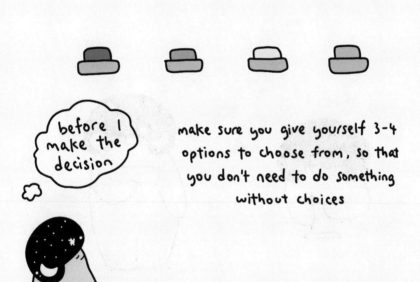

make sure you make yourself a priority
coz you are NOT less important than others

be aware of what you are cultivating
you deserve beautiful crops ♡

promise your heart you'll never let it go

share kindness to your heart
this is what your heart always does

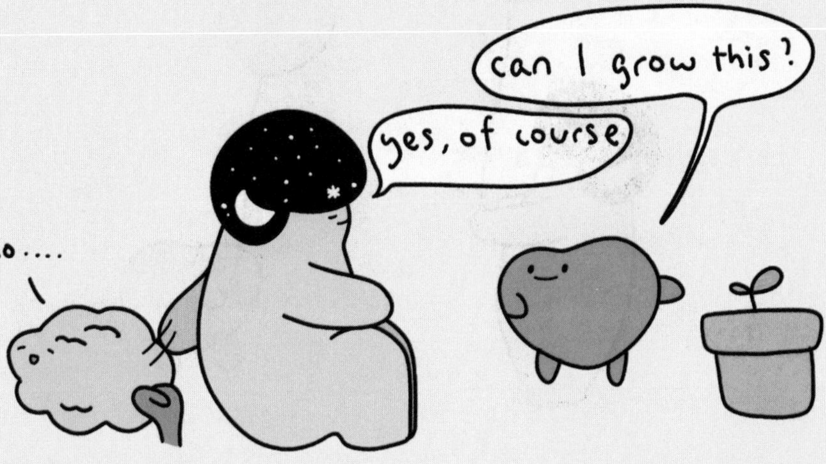
can I grow this?
yes, of course
no....

give yourself permission to do what you love

REMEMBER
you have a star to shine

maybe some people do not agree
with you, it's okay,
they are not the reason you shine

YOU ARE!!

setting boundaries is self-care

don't worry too much about what others think
it's not your job to fulfill everyone's requests

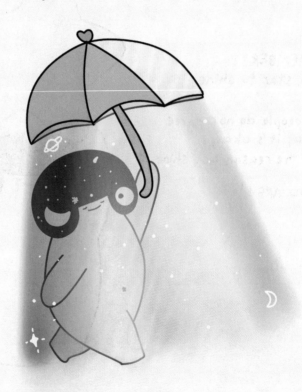

you are capable of making your dreams come true
keep creating what you want to see

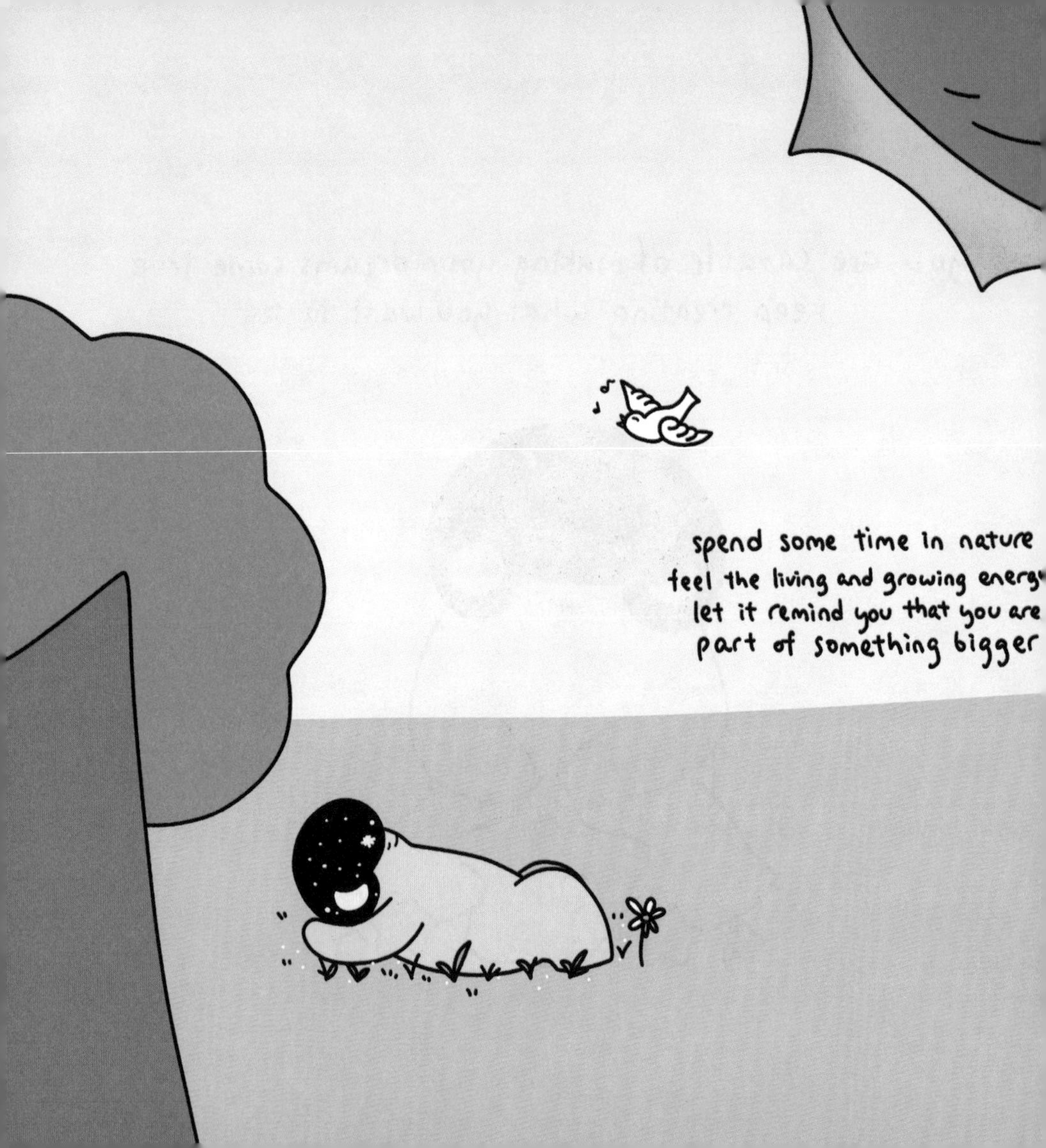
spend some time in nature
feel the living and growing energ
let it remind you that you are
part of something bigger

use this compass to guide you when you are lost

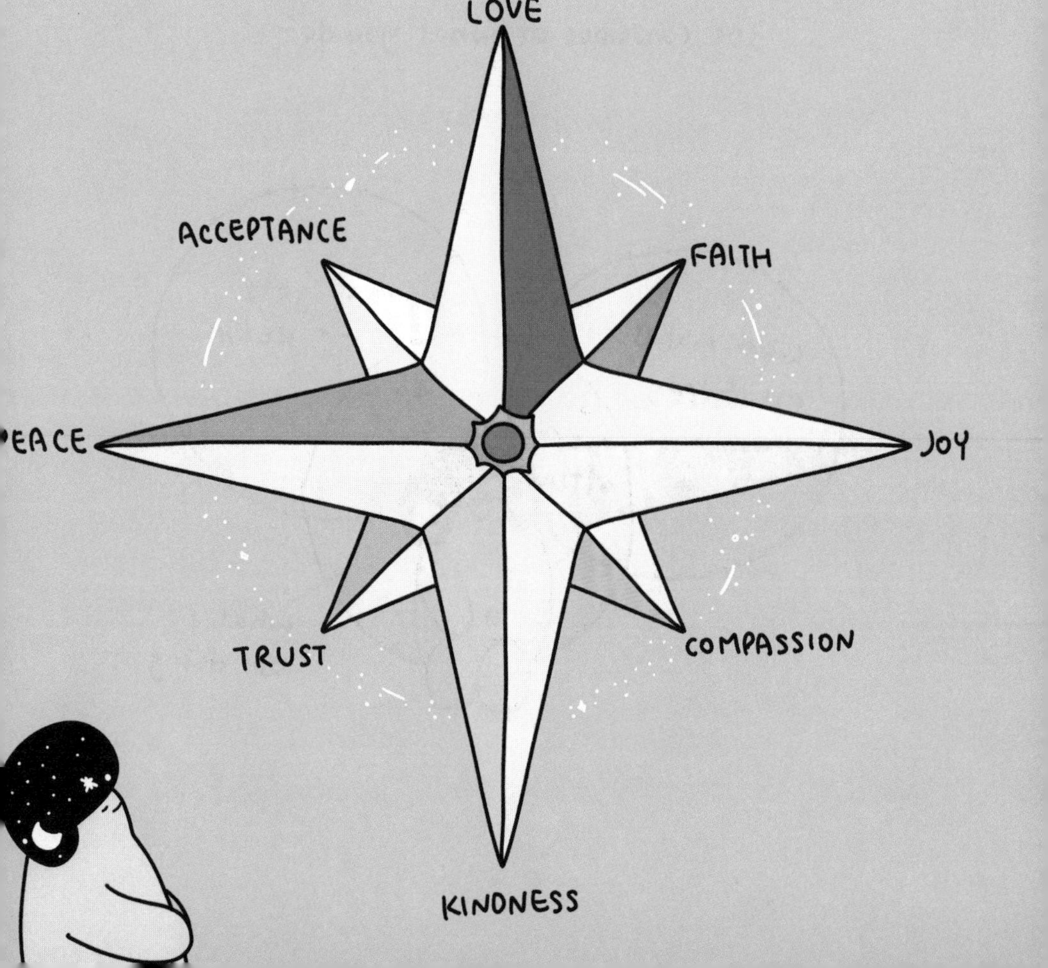
LOVE
ACCEPTANCE
FAITH
EACE
JOY
TRUST
COMPASSION
KINDNESS

be conscious of what you do

what makes me happy
what gets me down
do more often
do less
what I am doing

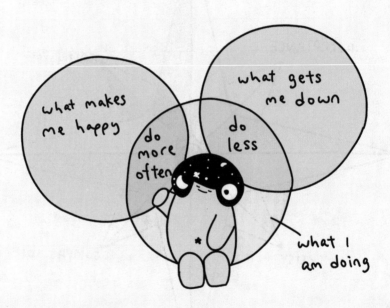

when you can only
see your shadow side,
please still give love

even your shadow needs love,
and then you'll see
your beautiful side again

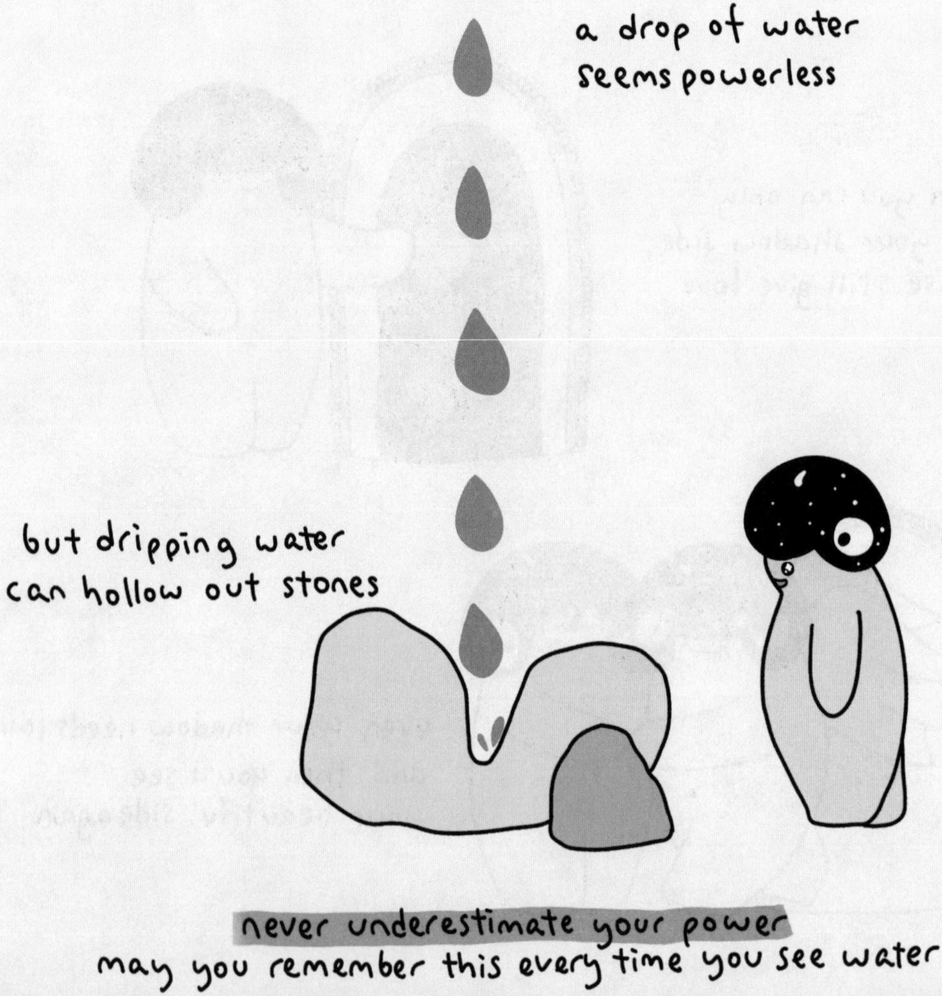
a drop of water
seems powerless
but dripping water
can hollow out stones
never underestimate your power
may you remember this every time you see water

YOU CAN ACHIEVE BIG GOALS

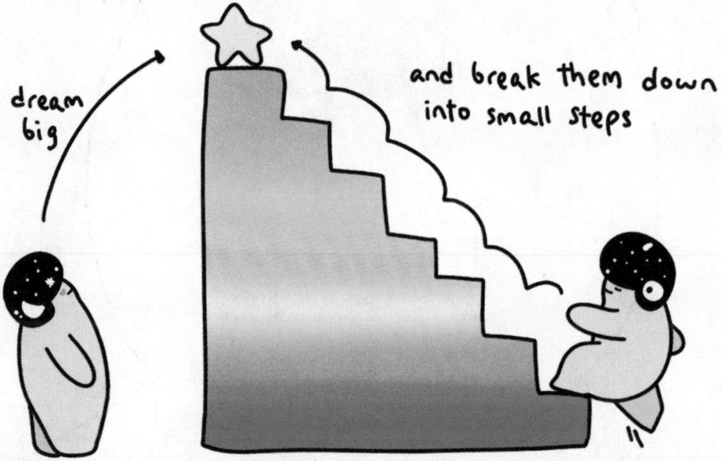
dream big
and break them down into small steps

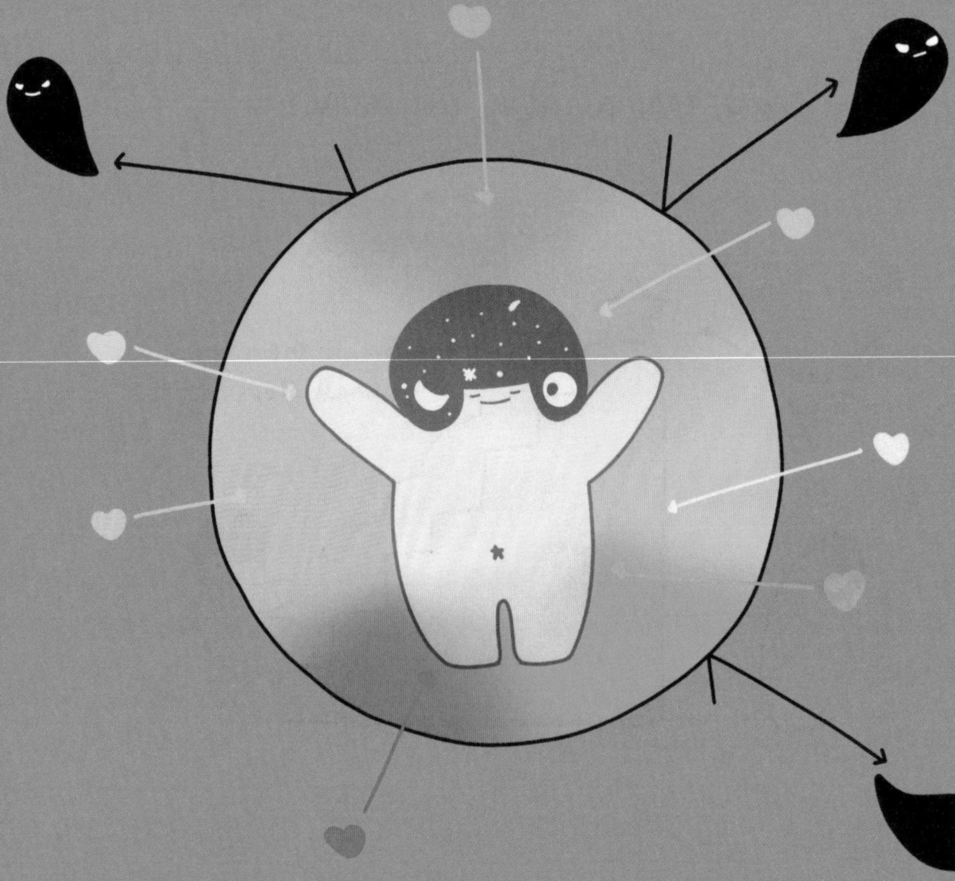

say no to what you don't want
and let what you want reach you

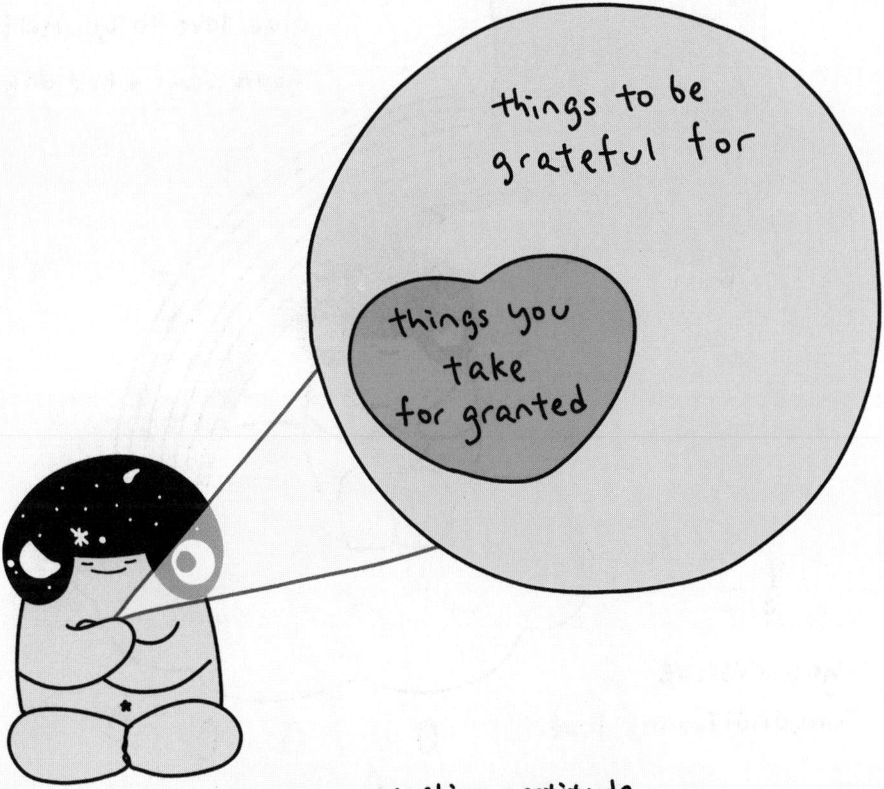
things to be grateful for
things you take for granted

practice gratitude

especially for things you take for granted

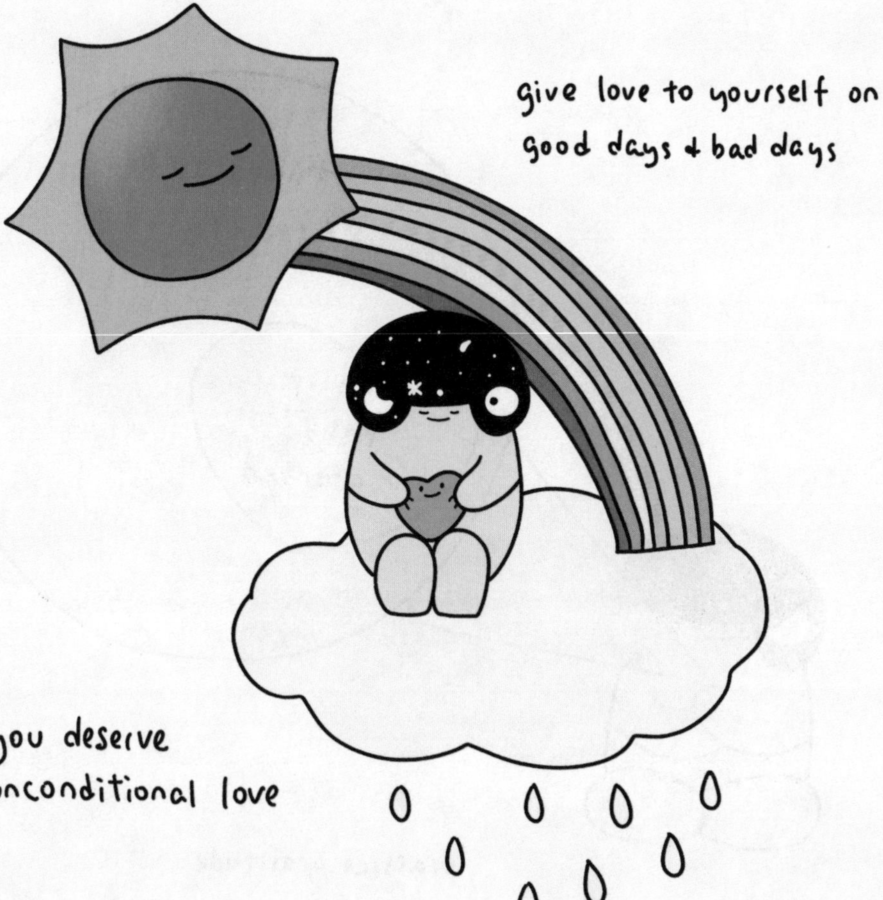
give love to yourself on
good days + bad days
you deserve
unconditional love

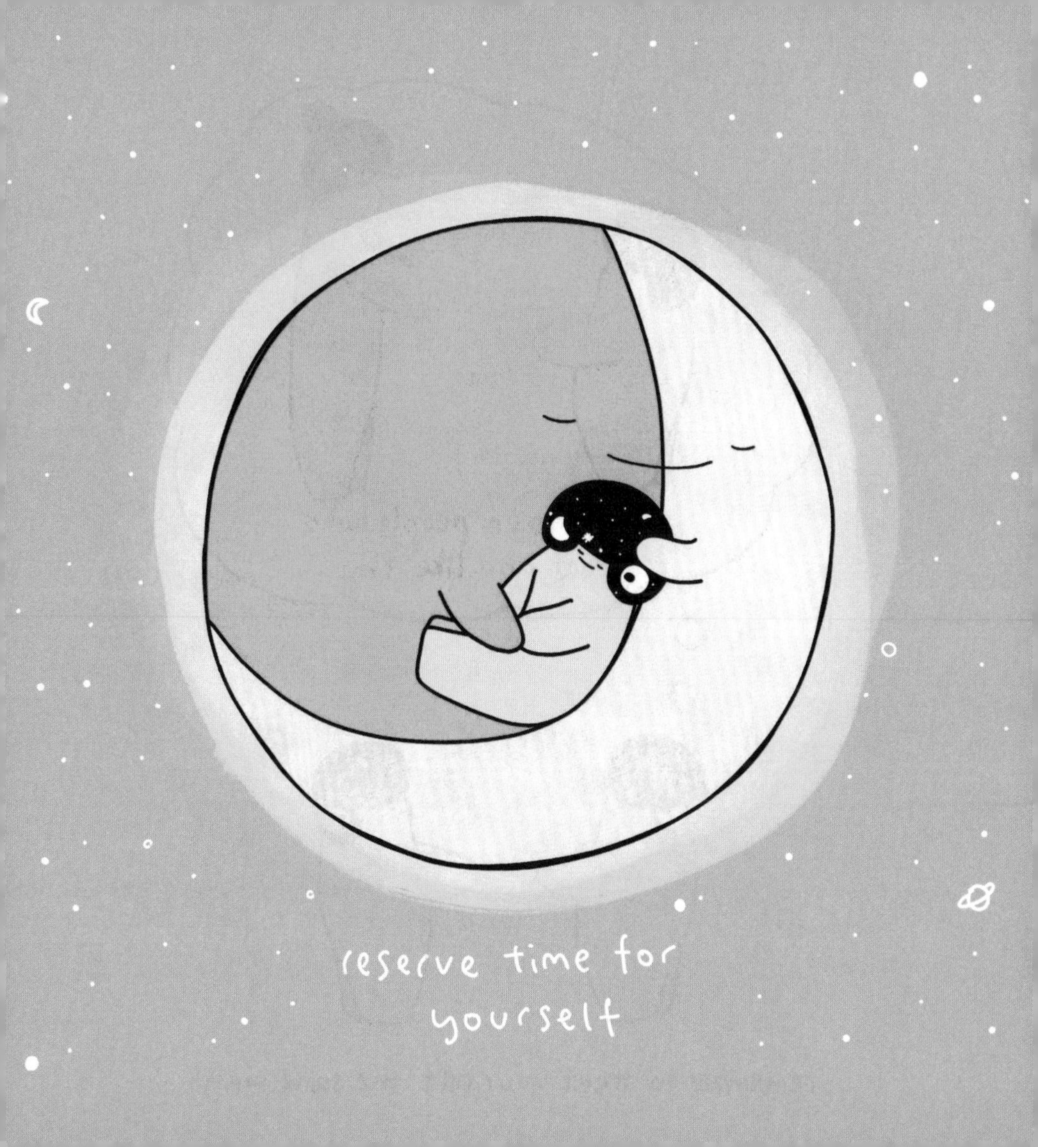
reserve time for
yourself

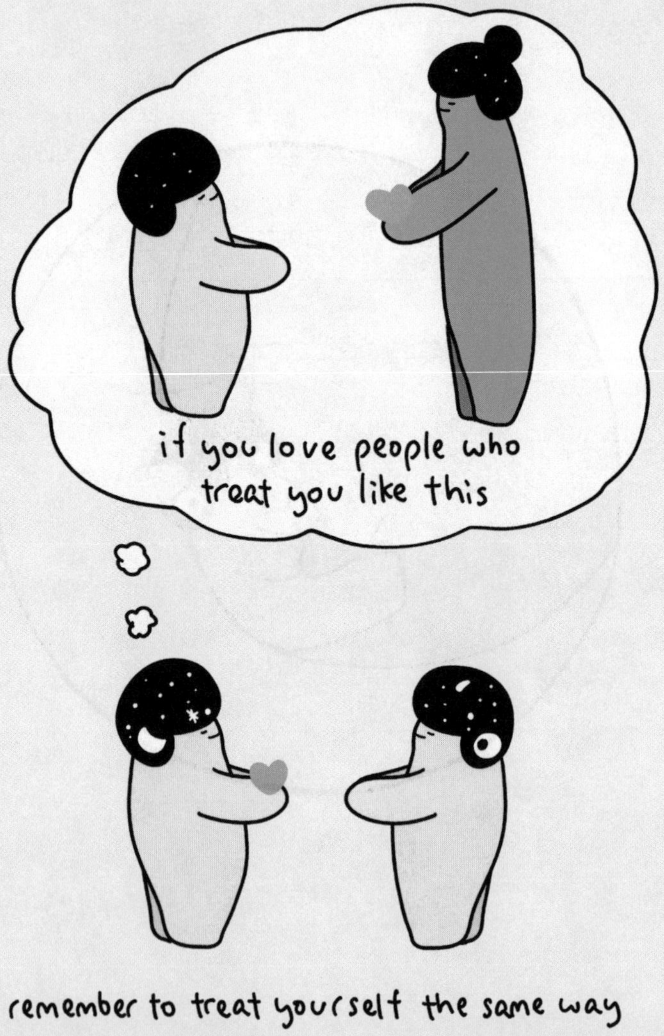
if you love people who
treat you like this
remember to treat yourself the same way

write down the things you would love your friends to do for you:

circle the things you are doing for your heart

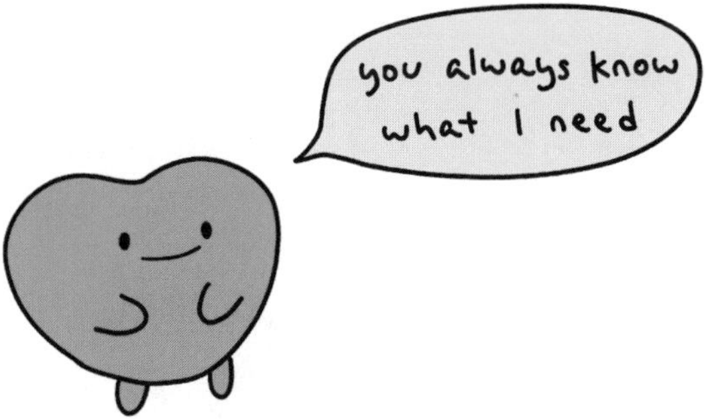
you always know what I need

Remember, there's no such thing called failure on the self-love journey. Whenever you think you've failed, pause. If you showed up—this is a success. If you tried—this is a success. If you think you failed because you have been trying so hard that you're exhausted—take a break. It's true that the journey can sometimes let you down. But you can never *fail* the journey, you just experience it.

Self-love may not be an easy task, but hating ourselves is not easy either. Ponder what your heart is yearning for. And commit to always be on your heart's side.

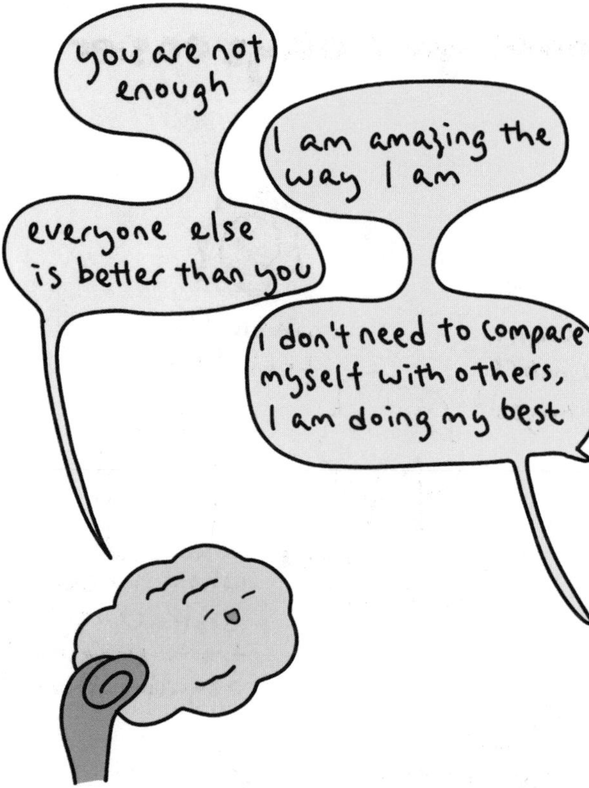
you are not enough
everyone else is better than you
I am amazing the way I am
I don't need to compare myself with others, I am doing my best

listen to your self-talk,
stand with and protect your heart

make a list of things that make your days easier

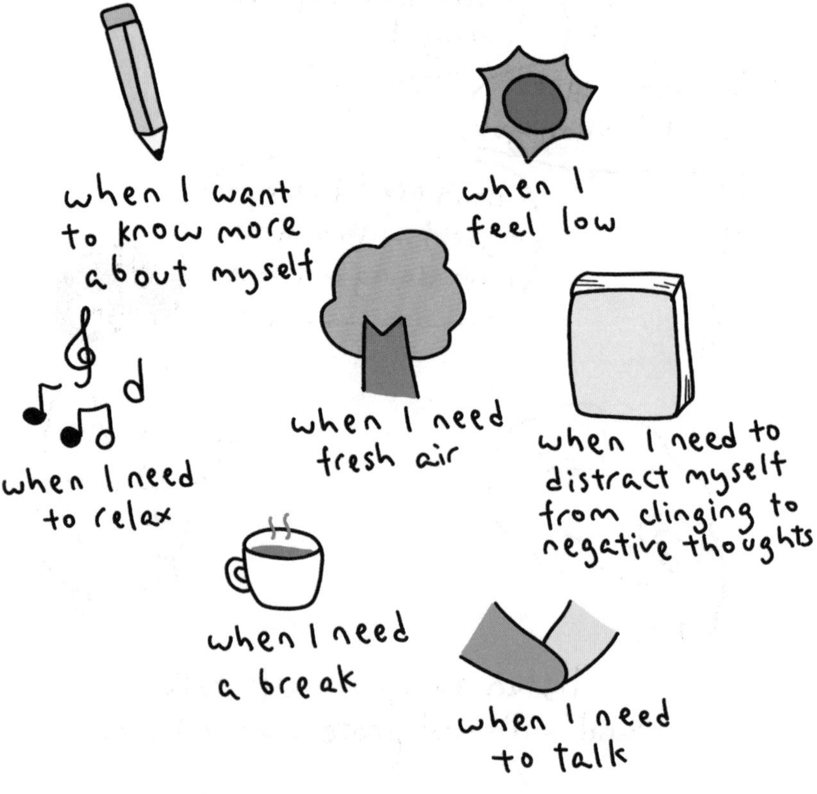

when I want to know more about myself
when I feel low
when I need fresh air
when I need to relax
when I need to distract myself from clinging to negative thoughts
when I need a break
when I need to talk

My List

of what makes my days easier

♥ _____

♥ _____

♥ _____

♥ _____

♥ _____

♥ _____

♥ _____

create your own affirmations

♥ _____

♥ _____

♥ _____

♥ _____

♥ _____

☆ use only positive words

☆ ☆ say them out loud, if you're comfortable with
   them, use them every day

CHAPTER SEVEN

AFFIRMATIONS

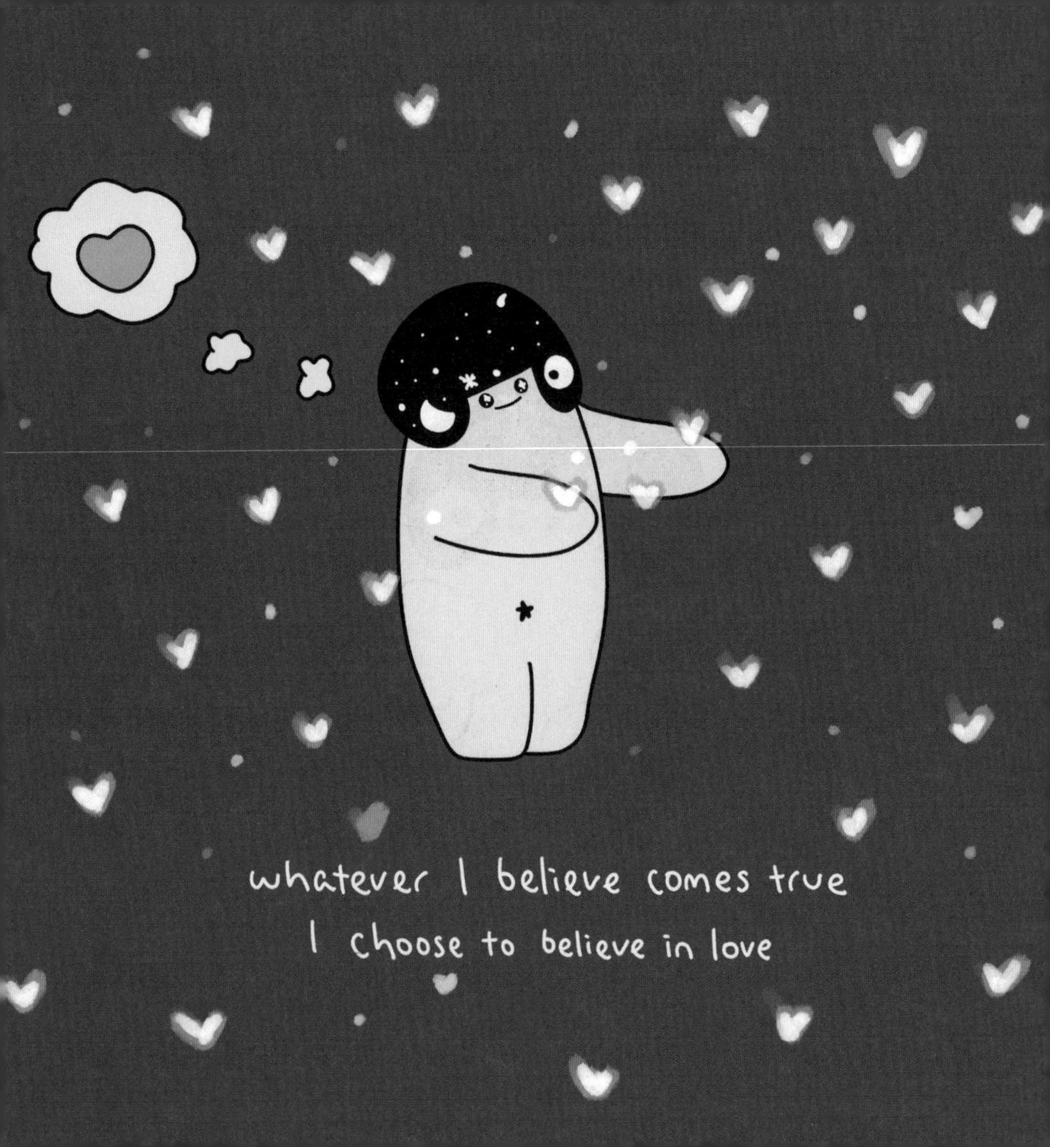
whatever I believe comes true
I choose to believe in love

I Believe in Me

I hope you have enjoyed this book so far, received the love I planted in it, and have seen the light within you. Just because we're getting to the end of the book doesn't mean it's the end of the journey, however.

Your self-love journey continues. Come back to the illustrations, exercises, and affirmations in this chapter and throughout the book whenever you need them. Soolooka is always here for you, in all circumstances.

Keep going. You know you can do it.

I live in the moment
everything will be okay

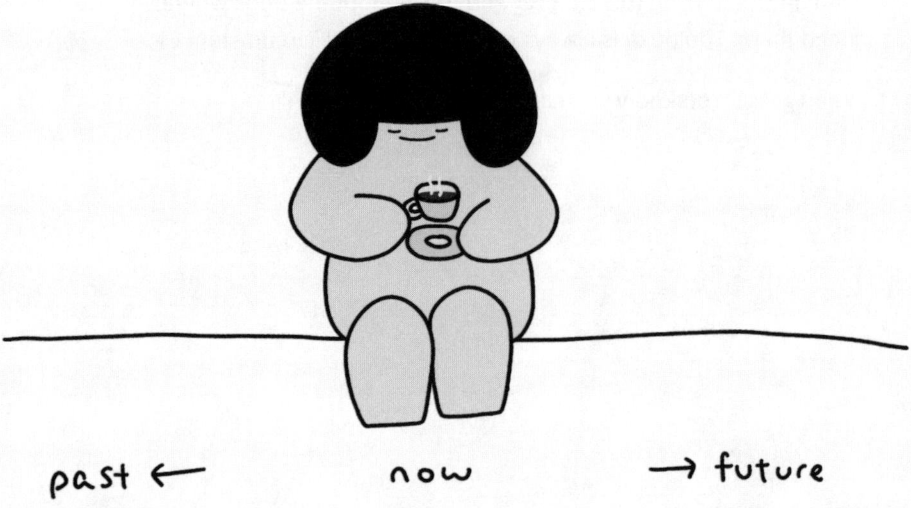

past ←
now
→ future

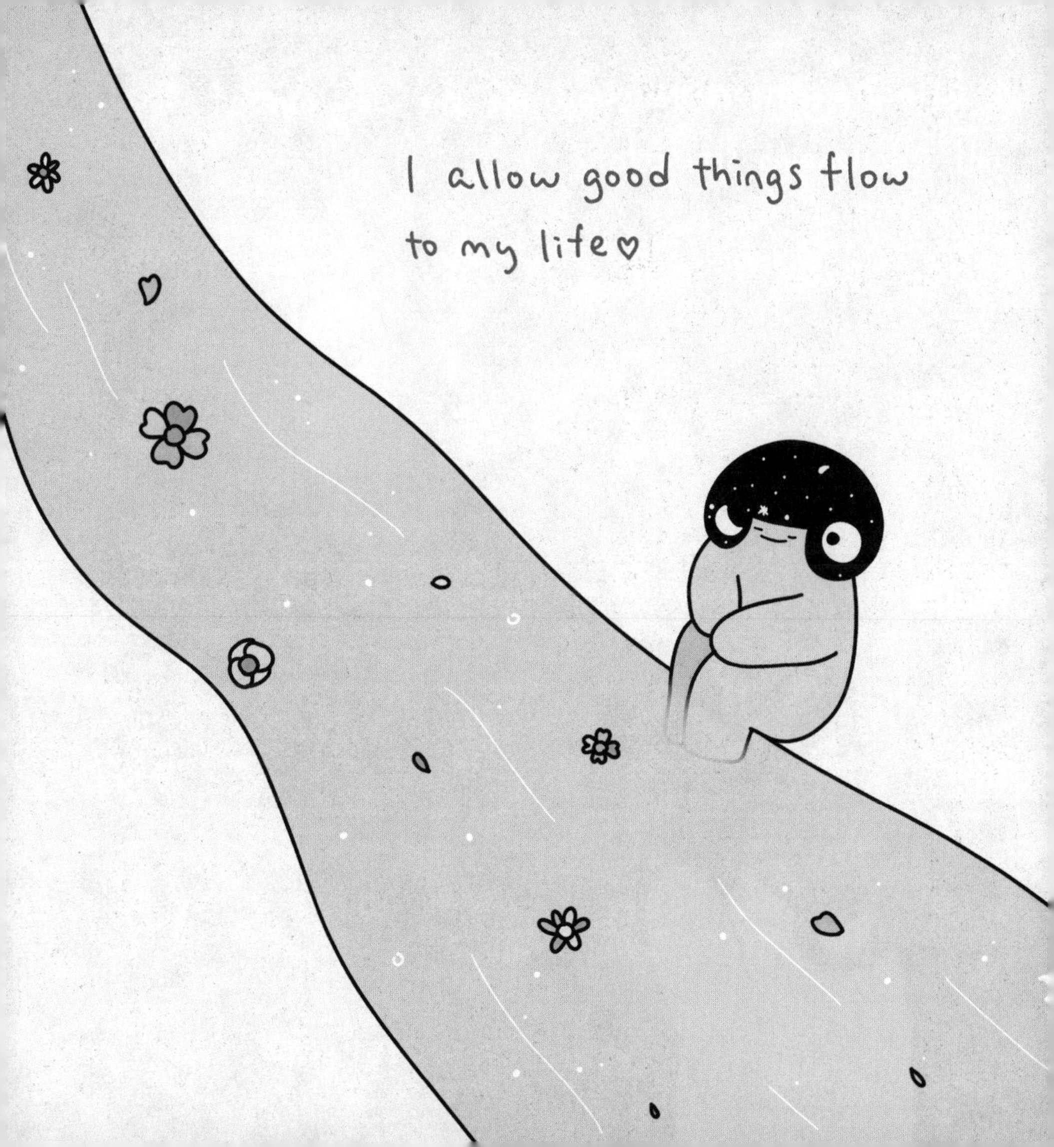
I allow good things flow
to my life♡

I allow my heart to show me the way out of all challenging situations

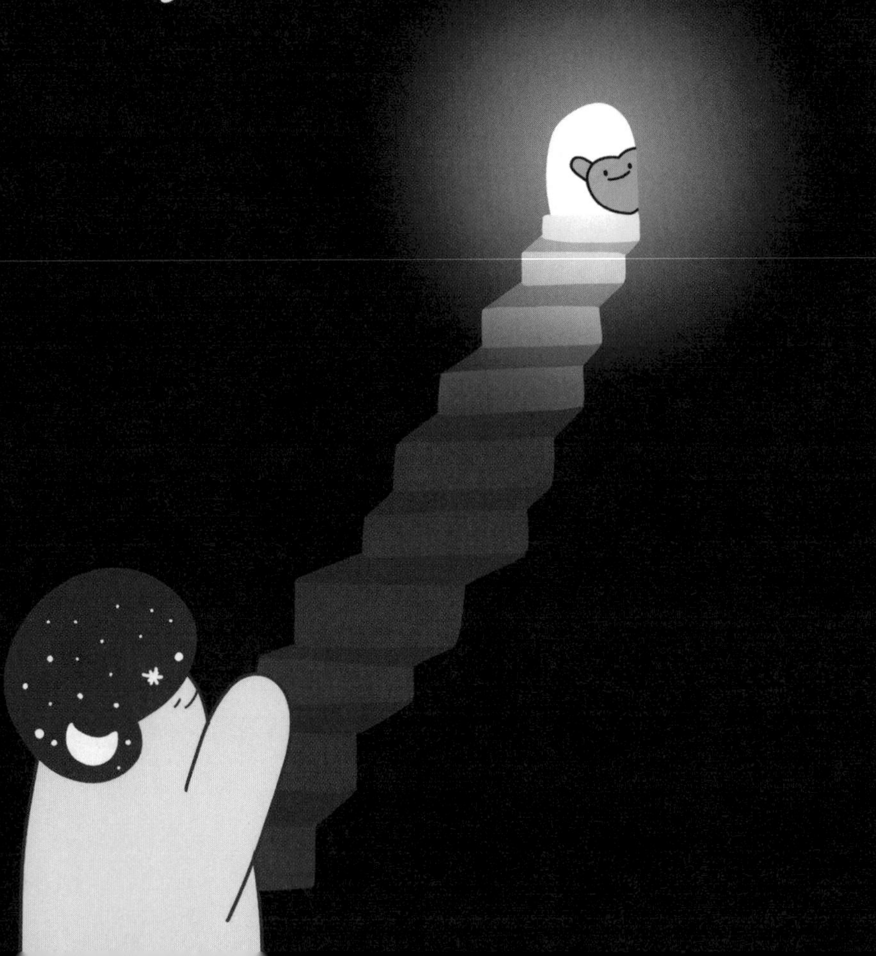

trust the process

everything I need comes to me at the right time

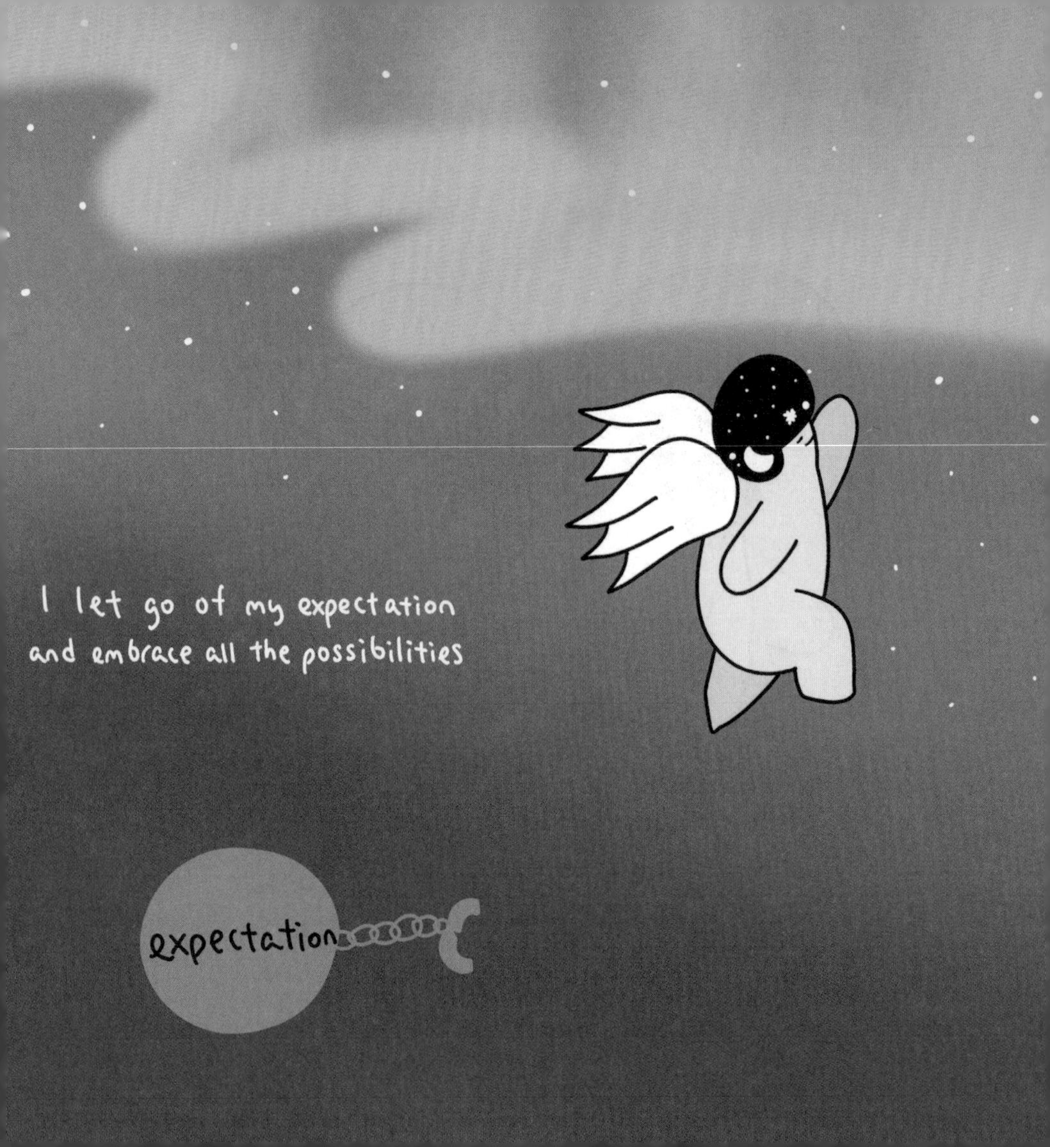
I let go of my expectation
and embrace all the possibilities
expectation

I am enough

I allow myself to radiate my light

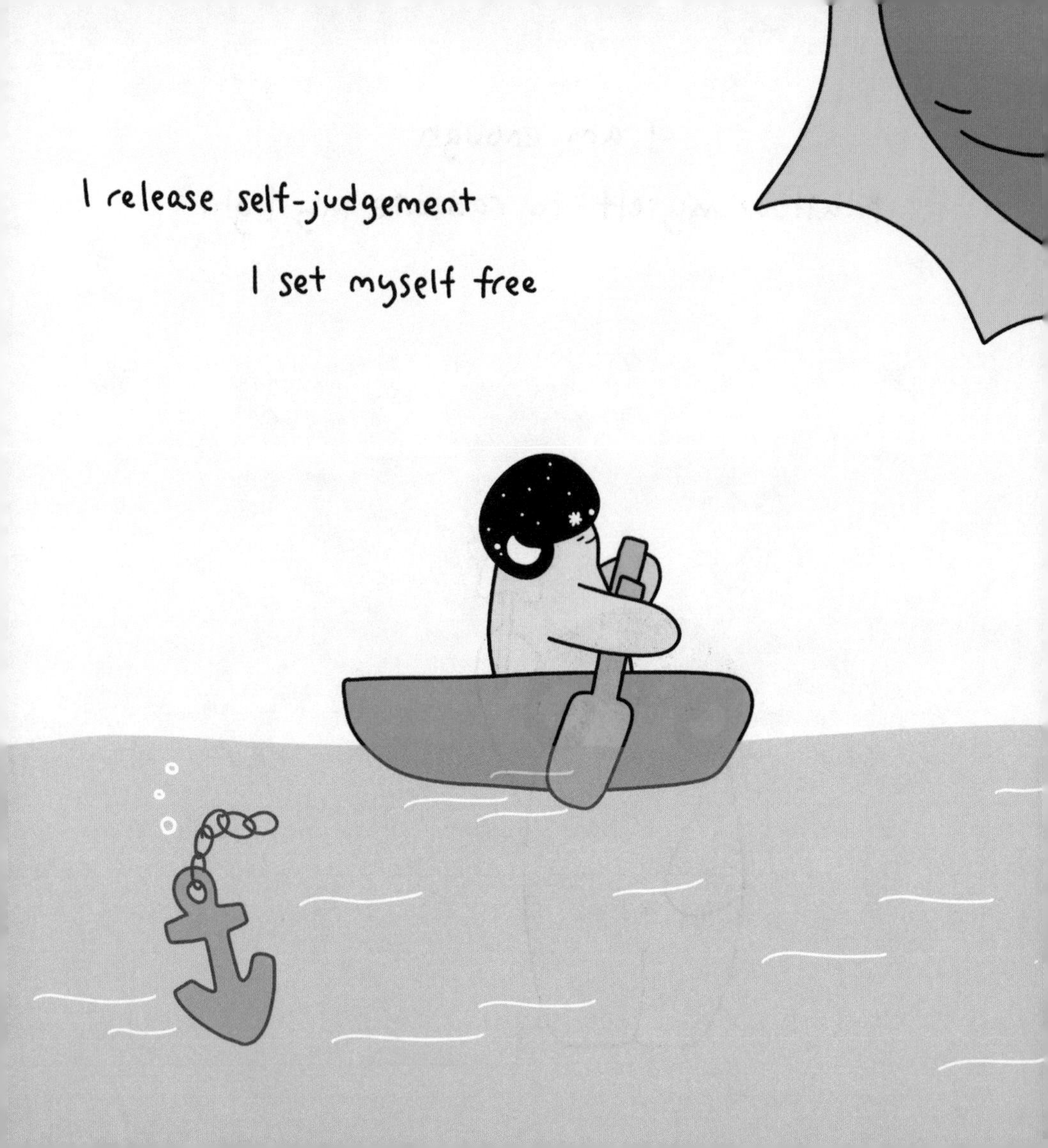
I release self-judgement
I set myself free

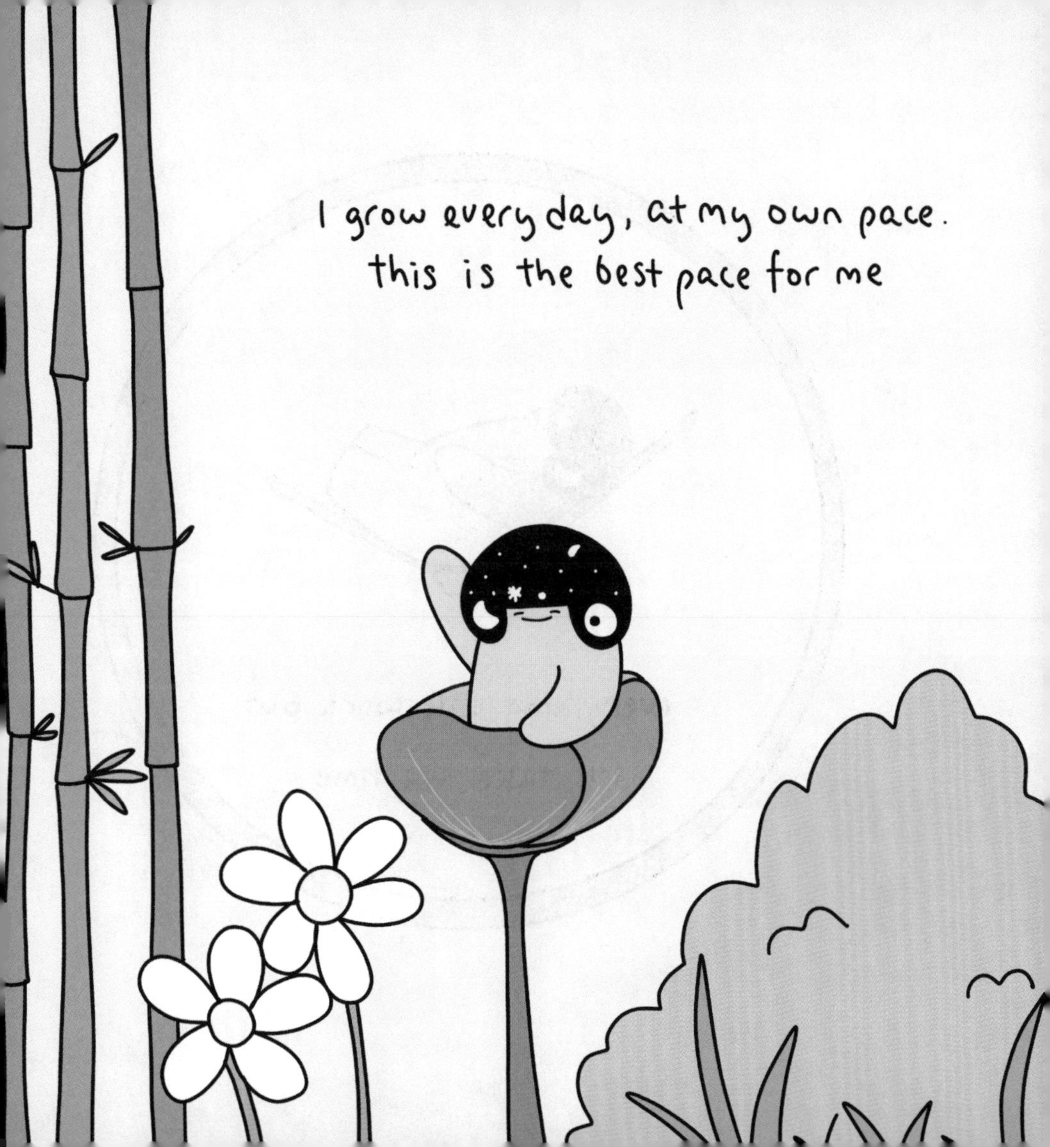
I grow every day, at my own pace.
this is the best pace for me

everything will work out
I'll take my time

I have faith
life has my back always

LIFE

I choose love
I accept love and I give love
love is always all around

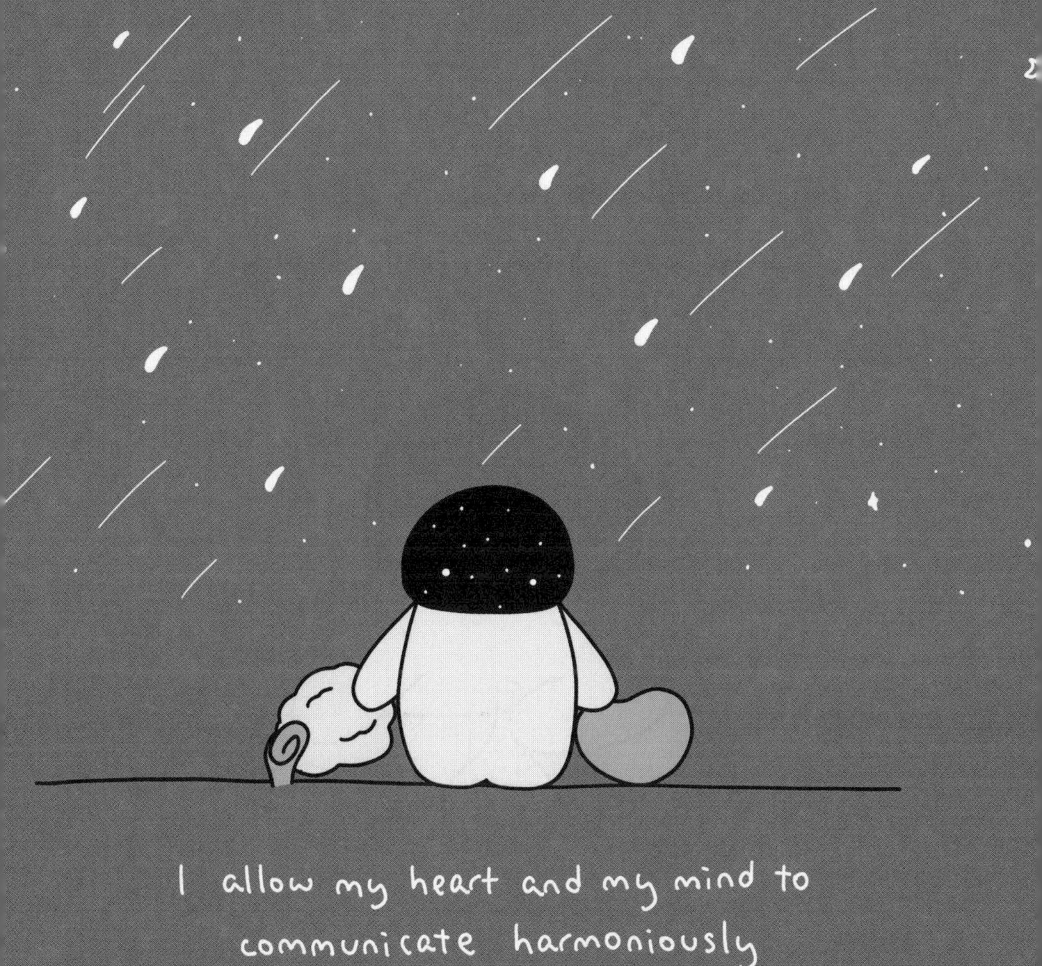

I allow my heart and my mind to
communicate harmoniously

I can create my own destiny,
with love, hope, and kindness

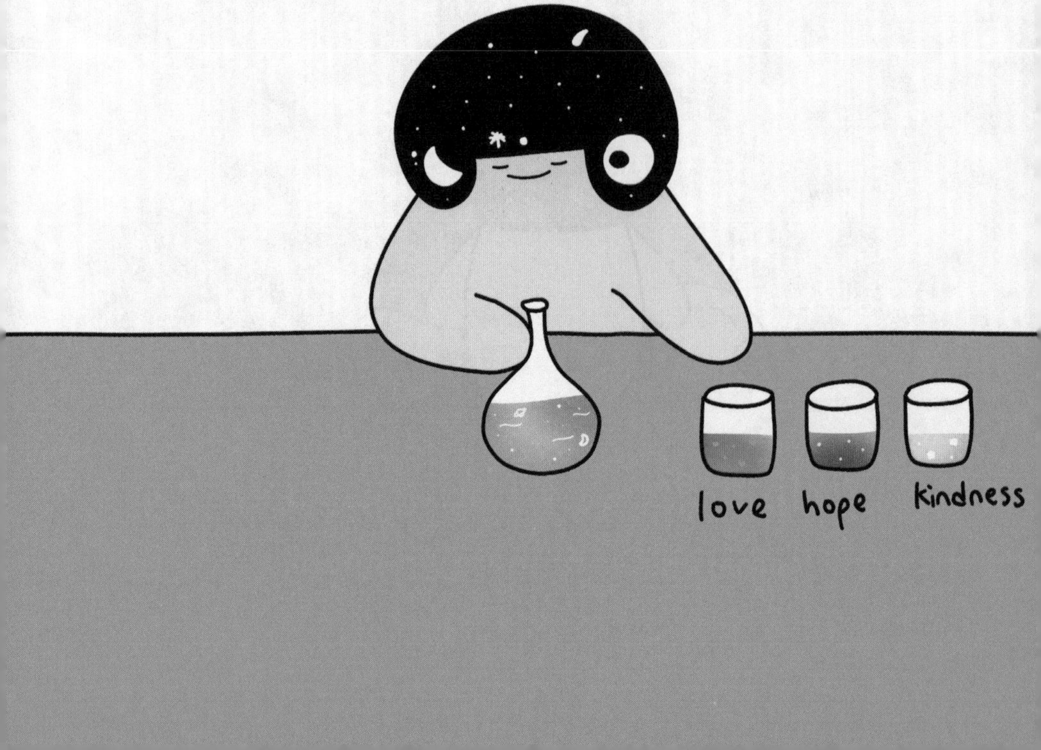
love
hope
kindness

I let the past be the past
I forgive myself
I am free to be who I want to be

I am lovable, just because

I deserve love and joy
I welcome them into my life

I say yes to my heart
I say yes to who I am

I am grateful for all I have

I always remember I am loved

as I let go of what doesn't serve m
everything is working for me

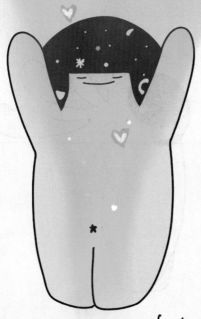

I am a vessel of love

I give love and receive love

whenever I speak,
I speak love, to others and myself

my happiness matters
I choose to focus on things that
make me happy

I allow myself to have enough rest

this helps me recharge

physically, emotionally, mentally, and spiritually

negative emotions are here
to tell me something.
I keep the messages
and let go of the
negative emotions

I approve of myself

I respect myself

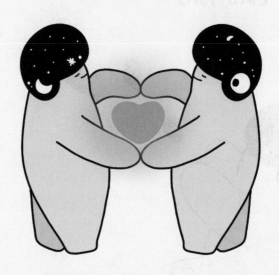

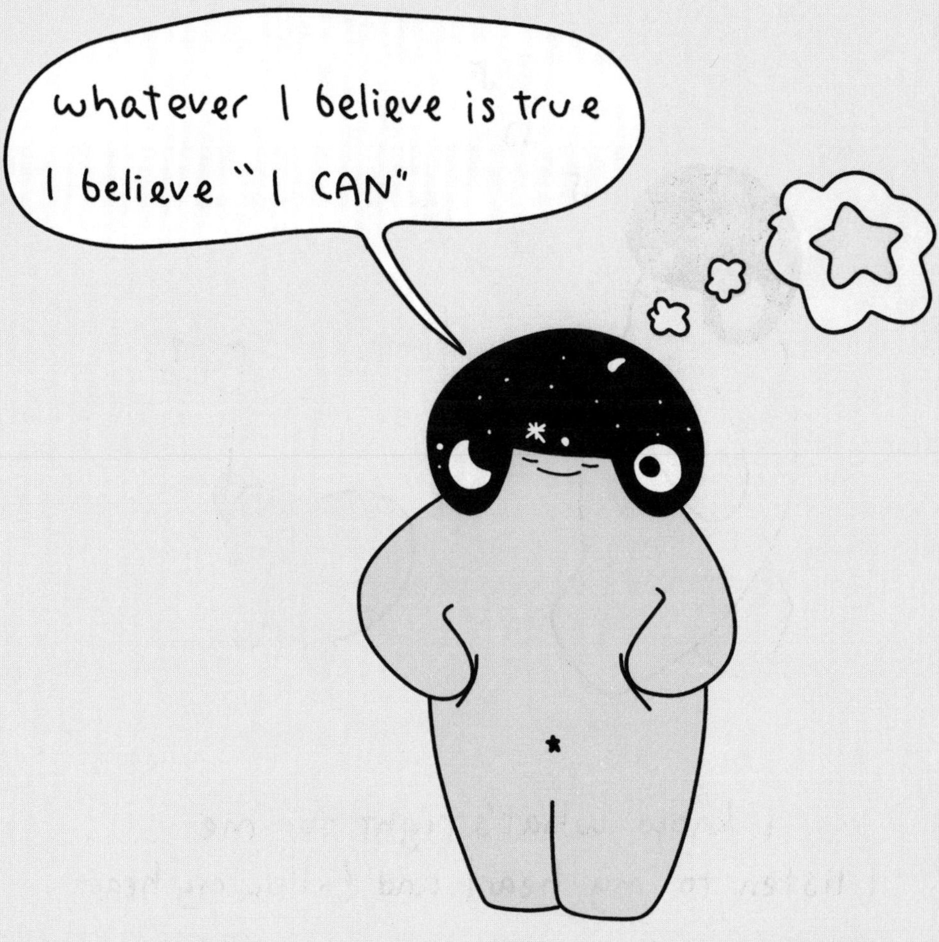
whatever I believe is true
I believe "I CAN"

I know what's right for me
I listen to my heart and follow my heart

I trust life

I let go of the need to control

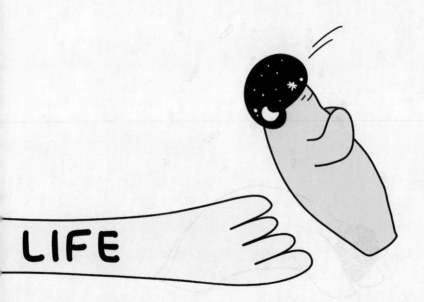

change is constant
I am flexible to adapt to changes

I am able to create positive thoughts

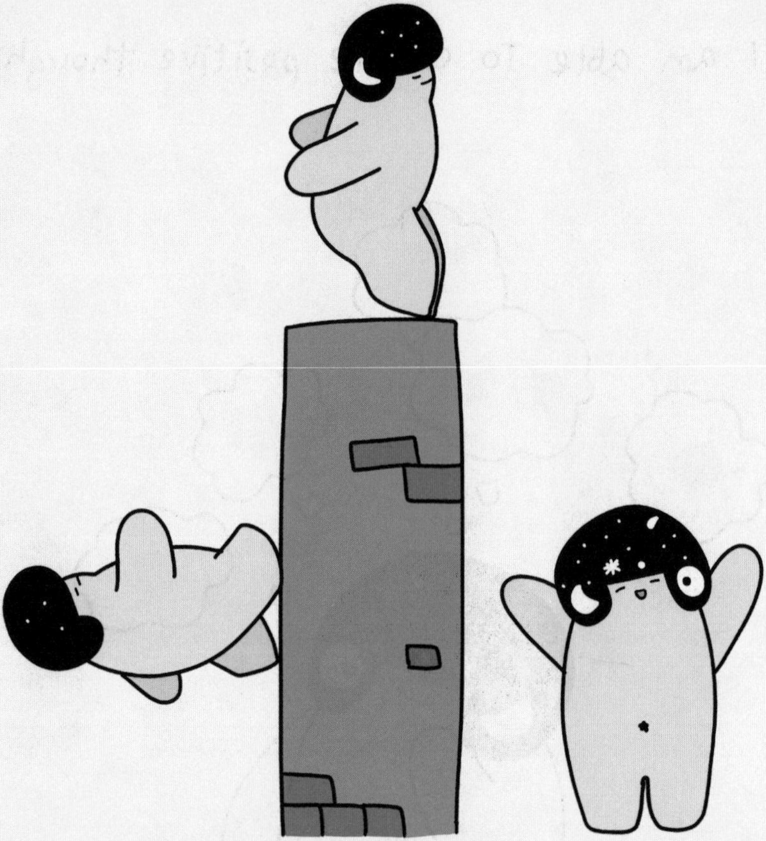

I am more powerful than my challenges

whenever I look into the mirror
I see a beautiful miracle

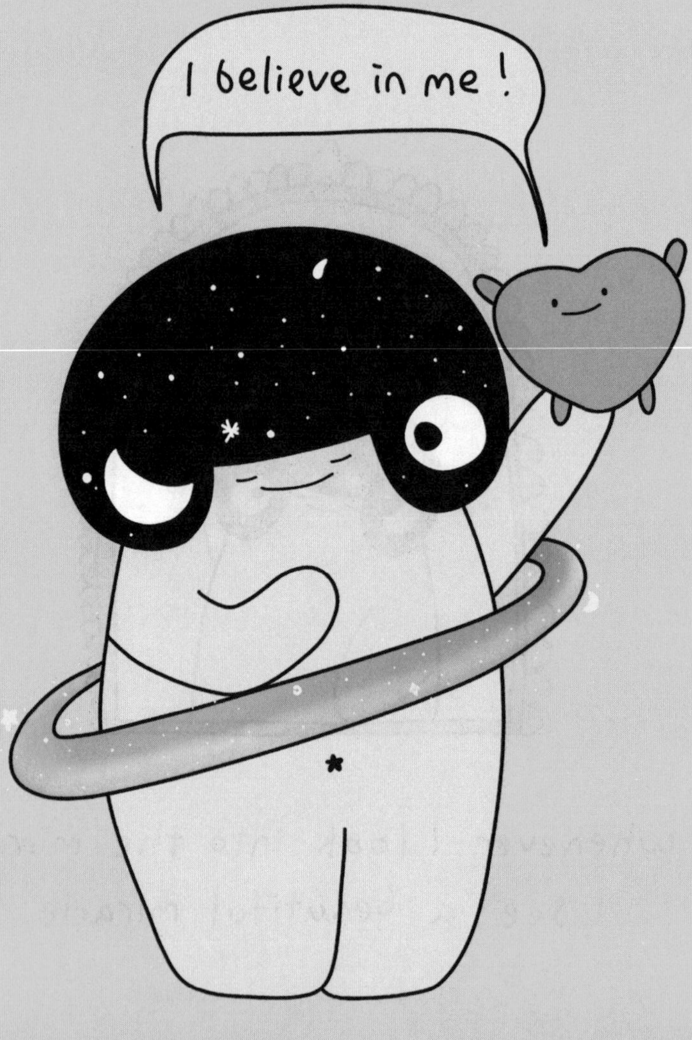
I believe in me!

Conclusion

Dear beautiful soul,

Thank you so much for joining the self-love journey with me, and including me in yours. Though self-love starts with the word "self," it doesn't mean your journey has to be lonely. There are times you need solitude, so that you can stop being distracting by the noise from the outside world, and start listening to yourself. However, there are times you need the company of others that makes you feel supported, and to support others in their self-love journey as well.

Self-love is both easy yet challenging. It is straightforward in that it can help you get through difficult times. But difficult when you're in a struggle against your negative thoughts and emotions on dark days—but you know you can get through them, as you always do. There is more than one way to perceive something, so find the viewpoint that makes your life more enjoyable.

I may not know your story, but I do know that it doesn't define who you are. You can always choose who you are, as well as who you are going to be.

One last thing—remember to thank yourself the most for all the efforts, tears, bravery, vulnerability you contribute. There will always be ups and downs in life, but at the end of it all, you will be okay. Believe in yourself!

Love,
Soolooka

Acknowledgments

I want to give a special thanks to my husband, Kevin Poon, who has supported me along this journey. He always encourages me to go for what I want to try, and made me the inspirational illustrator I am today. I am so grateful to have him in my life.

Another person I want to thank is Natasha Vera, my editor. She found me online when I had a very small following. She gave me the courage to do something bigger, even though I felt I wasn't famous enough. I really appreciate that she sees my star and helps me shine more brightly.

I would like to give a huge thanks to you, the special soul holding my book, and to my followers. Perhaps we haven't met in person, perhaps we haven't even chatted on social media, but you are my friends. And we've been connecting on a soul level since forever. Your love and support mean a lot to me and Soolooka.

About the Author

Cheng Chi Sing is the creator of Soolooka, and spreads self-love and self-care messages with cute characters on Instagram. She is a Reiki master who believes everyone deserves love and joy, and imagines there is a universe in everyone—full of beauty, wisdom, and magic. She thought she didn't know anything about drawing, but now dedicates her time to inspiring others with her fun and positive doodles.

Mango Publishing, established in 2014, publishes an eclectic list of books by diverse authors—both new and established voices—on topics ranging from business, personal growth, women's empowerment, LGBTQ studies, health, and spirituality to history, popular culture, time management, decluttering, lifestyle, mental wellness, aging, and sustainable living. We were recently named 2019 *and* 2020's #1 fastest growing independent publisher by *Publishers Weekly*. Our success is driven by our main goal, which is to publish high quality books that will entertain readers as well as make a positive difference in their lives.

Our readers are our most important resource; we value your input, suggestions, and ideas. We'd love to hear from you—after all, we are publishing books for you!

Please stay in touch with us and follow us at:

Facebook: Mango Publishing
Twitter: @MangoPublishing
Instagram: @MangoPublishing
LinkedIn: Mango Publishing
Pinterest: Mango Publishing

Sign up for our newsletter at www.mangopublishinggroup.com and receive a free book!

Join us on Mango's journey to reinvent publishing, one book at a time.

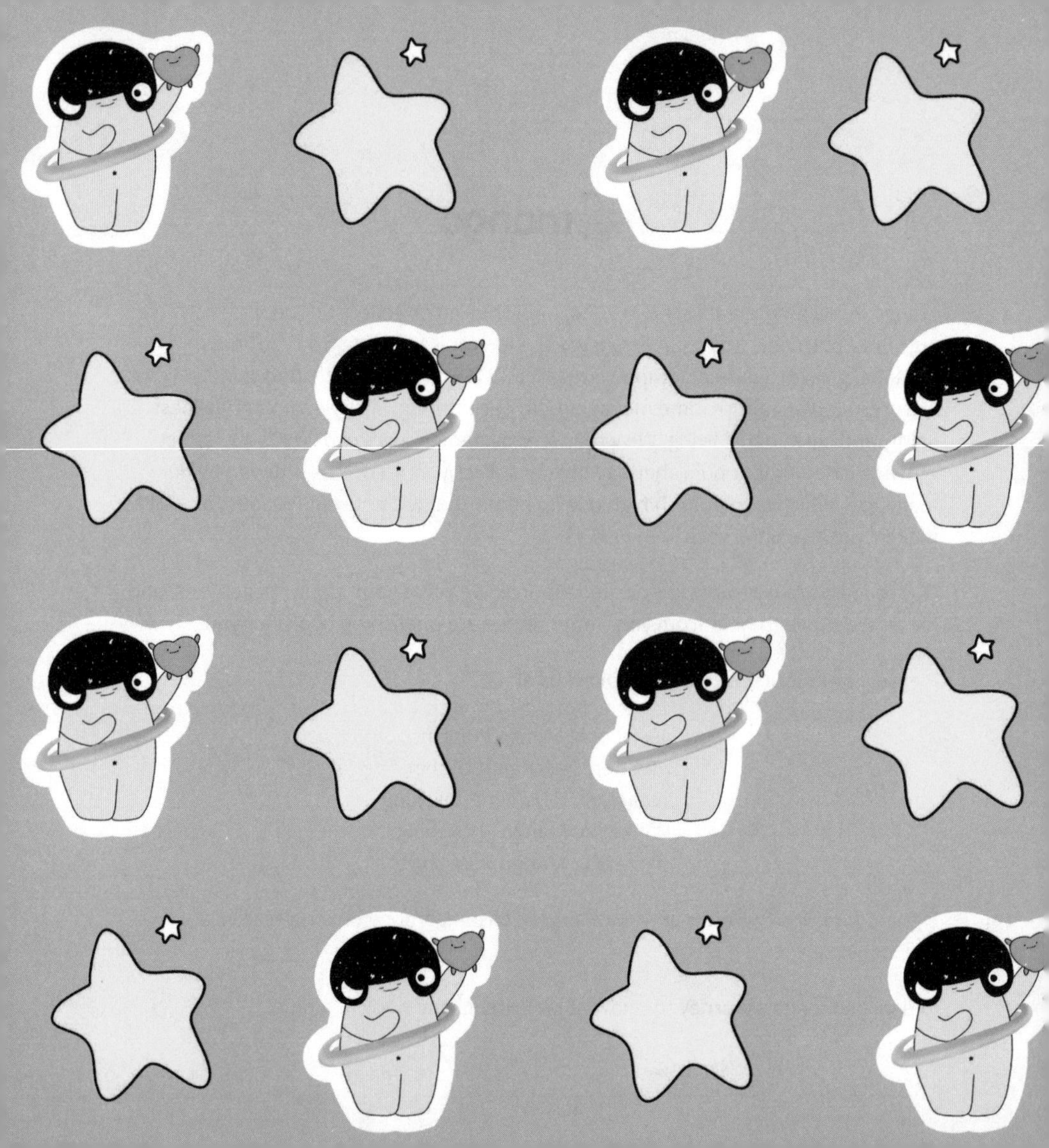